How to Make
Better Homebuying Decisions

An Insiders Guide to Help People Save Money & Avoid Costly Mistakes When Buying a Home

Resource Links: There are dozens of references to various resources, throughout the book, that the author feels would be helpful to the reader. They are presented throughout the book, at the end of the book in Appendix B and online at www.make-better-homebuying-decisions.com. The author would appreciate your help in keeping these resource links up-to-date by emailing him with any issues you find.

Published by: Tom Wemett, Homebuyer Advisors LLC, Post Office Box 72, Orange, MA 01364 Contact: (978) 248-9898 - Email Tom: tom@tomwemett.com

Cover design by: Vila Design - www.viladesign.net

ISBN Print Edition: 978-0-9995831-2-8

Table of Contents

Praise for "How To Make Better Homebuying Decisions" - *"It is essentially a consumer protection manual."*

Foreword - *"Tom's book takes apart and advises consumers about every aspect of a complicated home purchase process."*

Introduction - *"63% of millennial homeowners and 44% of all homeowners said they had buyer's remorse. They regretted buying their homes."*

Chapter One - Renting vs Owning - *"Stop Throwing Money Down the Drain. Five reasons why owning your own home makes more sense than renting."*

Chapter Two - Do You Have Enough Cash for a Down Payment and Closing Costs? - *"Ten ways to find cash for your down payment and closing costs."*

Chapter Three - Do You Have Credit Issues or Are Your Credit Scores Too Low? - *"Five ways to screw up your mortgage and home purchase."*

Chapter Four - Will You be Able to Find a Home You Like Within Your Budget? - *"Three steps to finding the right home within your budget."*

Chapter Five - Should You Wait to be in a Better Buying Position? - *"Don't throw caution to the wind and buy a home that you can't afford or that may not meet your basic needs or wants."*

Chapter Six - Do You Know Who to Trust and Work With? - *"The highest legal duty of one party to another is being a fiduciary. A real estate licensee can function as a true fiduciary like an attorney or they function as a salesperson playing, 'let's make a deal'."* Understand the difference!

Chapter Seven - Understanding Mortgage Options and Obtaining a True Mortgage Pre-approval - *"What is a loan estimate and why do you need one?"*

Chapter Eight - Looking at All Available Homes - *"It is vital that you know the local market. You must develop an intuitive feeling for value."*

Chapter Nine - Developing a Negotiating Strategy Before Making an Offer - *"Thirteen Tips for determining a starting offer price."*

Chapter Ten - Including Contingencies for Property Inspections - *"Know the home you are buying. For Your Protection: Get a Home Inspection."*

Chapter Eleven - Knowing What Other Contingencies to Include in Your Offer - *"Eleven important contract contingencies helpful for a buyer."*

Chapter Twelve - Continuing to Check and Follow Up - *"Eleven action items that need attention for a successful home closing."*

Chapter Thirteen - Preparing for and Foreseeing Problems at Closing Time - *"There still is much to do once the closing date is set."*

Chapter Fourteen - Closing and Moving-In - *"Closings often become battlegrounds. Don't let that happen to you."*

Appendix A - Buying a Home During a Pandemic & Economic Crisis - *"You may want to reconsider your own personal safety and economic well-being if you are actively out looking to buy a home right now while a national pandemic continues to rage."*

Appendix B - Resources Link Summary - *"Find direct links to websites and other resources mentioned throughout the book."*

About the Author - *"Homebuyers want to buy the right home at the right price. Tom's focus is to make sure that happens and has dedicated his real estate career to that goal."*

Other books by Tom Wemett - Available at Amazon.com

Massachusetts Homebuyers Beware! The Cards are Stacked Against You. - *"The author helps flip the odds in favor of the homebuyer, provides information that will help the homebuyer buy the right home at the right price, and provides the homebuyer with knowledge to enable finding the right agent."*

Not One Dollar More! How to Save $3000 to $30000 Buying Your Next Home - Collaborating Author with Joseph Cummins - *"Almost all homebuyers pay too much for their homes - and never discover their misfortune! After all, who's going to tell you? Think about it. Since 1995 this book has helped over 100,000 homebuyers to save money, avoid tricks and traps, buy safely the RIGHT home and get true peace of mind."*

Praise for *How to Make Better Homebuying Decisions*

If I were buying a home in the author's area I would not hesitate for one second to engage his services.

If that were not possible, I'd search out his advice. And if I could not obtain his advice directly, I'd make sure to read what he writes.

Every buyer in the US can now have access to that advice for the cost of two cups of coffee.

If there has ever been a better bargain for the homebuyer, I don't know of it.

Despite all the hype you'll hear, it's rare that any expert writes a book that can save the reader thousands of dollars, potentially tens of thousands. Not to mention the peace of mind that comes from knowing you bought the right home at the right price.

This is one of those rare books.

It is essentially a consumer protection manual. Here, the consumer that needs protection and guidance is you, the homebuyer.

You might not appreciate that at this moment. Reading just a few pages will convince you otherwise. Whether you are buying your first home or your fifth makes no difference — you have a lot to lose when you are unaware of how homebuying really works (most buyers are in this bracket).

I only wish I had Tom Wemett by my side in 1995 when I wrote the first edition of *Not One Dollar More!: How to Save $3,000 to $30,000 Buying Your Next Home*. At that time, few homebuyers were aware that they had no one looking out for them when they went about buying a home.

The vast majority of buyers put their full trust in the local real estate salesperson, believing that this salesperson would honor their trust, keep all their personal information confidential, and negotiate the best deal on their behalf.

But that could not be.

Few selling agents explained that to do this would be illegal (and still is). They did not make clear that they were obligated by law to get the best deal, best price, and best terms — not for the homebuyer! — but for the seller. And *only* for the seller.

Traditional selling agents are still bound by these same (fiduciary) laws.

Test this out. Next time you go house hunting ask the agent: *'Will you commit to representing my best interests, and only my best interests, at all times?'* Then note the response you get. This book explains what to do next.

When *Not One Dollar More!* was first published it blew the cover on such systemic deception. Some real estate professionals were so disturbed that a number of them thought it appropriate to phone me and issue very serious threats.

At the time, I was researching as a consumer advocate but had previous hands-on experience in real estate. So, in Washington DC I sought the input of lawmakers and consumer advocates, including Ralph Nader and Stephen Brobeck, both of whom, along with others, supported fair and separate representation for the homebuyer. My research for *Not One Dollar More!* started out as my PhD dissertation project, which changed with my decision to publish it as a how-to book for homebuyers.

Today, homebuyers need protection every bit as much as they did then. In short, every homebuyer needs an advocate, a true and genuine ally who is not operating underhandedly, not surreptitiously serving the best interests of the other side. And not serving the best interest of neither side, which, incredibly, still goes on.

For you, the homebuyer, the agent you want working for you is what the author refers to as an Exclusive Buyer Agent or Single-Party Agent - a True Loyal Agent(R). This is your 100% advocate, your trustworthy confidant. This book shows you how to locate and engage such an agent.

Whether you take this route or not, the author helps you become what I have always called a 'smart homebuyer' (a tiny minority of buyers). As a smart buyer you know how to avoid the traps that steal your money, and not just that. You also know how to make sure you don't regret your purchase when it's too late, when you are stuck with a house you don't want — perhaps the 'house from hell'.

Of course, this guide helps you do a lot more than finding and buying the right home at the lowest possible price and on the best terms.

It explains how to get the least expensive home loan, *what* you need to do, *when* you need to do it, and *how*. Also, how to work your credit score to keep extra dollars in your pocket every month. And a whole lot besides (take a peek at the Contents page).

I know a good bit about real estate. But I don't know all that Tom Wemett knows — not even nearly. In truth, he is the most knowledgeable expert on real estate matters that I have met. Along with that, he has been dedicated solely to *your* best interests — the homebuyer — for three decades.

Earlier, I said I would not hesitate to engage the author if I were buying a home in his area.

Two years ago I went even further. Out of potentially hundreds of willing experts, I chose Tom Wemett to collaborate with me on the third edition of *Not One Dollar More!*. Fortunately, he agreed, and we released the entirely re-written and updated new edition, which reached #1 on Amazon.

Finally, homebuying can be a minefield — though the dangers are rarely made clear, especially to first-time buyers. With this book in hand, you will stand the best chance of getting just the right home, at the lowest possible price, on the best terms available, along with the best financing.

I expect that's exactly what you'll do. *Joseph Éamon Cummins, Consumer Advocate and Organizational Psychologist - (August 2020)*

Foreword

I am a consumer advocate who, for nearly three decades, has sought to expose and reform conflicts of interest endemic to our real estate brokerage marketplace. Tom is a real estate broker who is obligated to function within this marketplace. So why did I agree to write this preface? There are two compelling reasons.

First, Tom is extremely knowledgeable and objective about real estate issues. He is usually the first person I consult when trying to better understand the real estate marketplace. This knowledge and objectivity can be seen in every chapter of How to Make Better Homebuying Decisions. I could not find an important issue that he did not insightfully address.

Second, Tom is an effective advocate for the buyers he represents. Early in his career, Tom recognized the inevitable conflicts of interest that arose from working with both home buyers and sellers. How could he adequately represent buyers when he had listings whose sellers also deserved good representation? Would not he be forced either to promote these listings to his buyers or neglect the interests of his sellers? To his great credit, Tom realized he could not be a "True Loyal Agent(R)" to both at the same time, so decided to represent only buyers as an "exclusive buyer broker."

Tom's book takes apart and advises consumers about every aspect of a complicated home purchase process, from contemplation of home ownership to the house closing. He also makes good suggestions about obtaining a mortgage and seeking the assistance of a real estate lawyer.

Throughout the book there are two themes. One is to plan carefully – take time to consider all important aspects of qualifying for and selecting a mortgage, choosing a real estate agent, selecting a home, and getting good value for the sale price. A home purchase is, for most families, the most important consumer decision they will make in their lifetime. This choice could well greatly advance their long-term economic security or create huge financial problems. It could provide a wonderful environment in which to live and raise a family, or it could result in numerous irritations and dissatisfactions.

The second theme is to seek the assistance of a highly competent agent, loyal only to you, who can help you understand and make good decisions at all stages of the home-buying process. This agent should not agree to represent you, then promote one of their listings or those of their firm. Instead, this agent should agree to show you any property in which you are interested. This agent should also give you good information and wise advice that builds your confidence, not your anxiety. This agent should help you efficiently obtain good value in your home purchase.

As Tom cautions, the current Covid-influenced home marketplace is especially fraught with risk, so good planning and loyal representation are even more important. Yet, despite the current crisis, as a nation we will eventually meet these challenges. As we do, How to Make Better Homebuying Decisions will become even more useful to more Americans. *Stephen Brobeck, Senior Fellow, Consumer Federation of America - (August 2020)*

Introduction

A Quick Note:

This book is written from the perspective of a true homebuyer advocate and not a salesperson. It will show you how to save money and protect your best interests during the homebuying process. Buying a home in the traditional way, using a real estate salesperson, may not be as safe as you think.

I explain the concept of True Loyal Agent(R) in Chapter Six, but I will quickly explain it here.

A True Loyal Agent(R) can be an exclusive buyer agent. Exclusive buyer agents represent buyers only and never represent sellers or take listings. They are with a real estate company that never represents sellers and never takes listings.

A True Loyal Agent(R) can also be a single-party agent. Single-party agents represent buyers and sellers but never in the same transaction. They never do an in-house deal where agents in the same real estate company attempt to represent both a buyer and a seller on the same property.

Why it matters will be explained in detail in Chapter Six including how to find one. But for now, understand that I am not a real estate salesperson. As an exclusive buyer agent for the last 28 years I always look out for a homebuyer's best interest. That is the basis for my writing this book.

So with that said, let's begin.

Has this happened to you?

- You drive home to your apartment after work. There is someone parked in your designated parking space. The only space available seems like a mile walk from your apartment.

- You come home to your apartment dead tired. You want to relax but the neighbor's dog is barking. Another neighbor's baby is crying for what seems like forever.

- The landlord won't come and fix that plumbing leak or the non-working burners on the stove. You have been telling him about these for at least two months.

- The landlord did let you know that your rent is going up by $150 per month starting in a month.

I'm sure you have similar stories to tell if given a chance.

At the end of the year the only thing you have to show for your rent payments for the year is a stack of rent receipts. You can't even write them off or get a deduction off your income taxes for the thousands of dollars you spent.

Is it time to reconsider renting?

Have you had enough of throwing money down the drain?

Are you feeling trapped renting?

Are you dreaming about owning your own home and getting out of apartment renting for good?

Are you looking for:

- Control over your living space?

- The opportunity to build financial assets in the form of equity in your home?

- Saving through income tax benefits?

- Potential lower housing expense long term with fixed monthly mortgage payments vs. increasing rent payments.

- A pride of ownership feeling?

- A place of your own in which to raise a family?

These are a few of the benefits of owning your own home.

These ideals prompted one of my clients to take action.

Betsy and Andrew were plain tired of paying rent. They had nothing to show for it but canceled rent checks. On the way to the grocery store, Andrew saw an open house sign. It had a bunch of balloons tied to it with lots of cars in the driveway. He decided to take a peek. It was perfect for them. He made an appointment with the real estate agent for him and Betsy to go back the very next day!

They made an offer. The seller agreed to accept it. They told their friends. They wanted to buy that home, but would they get approved for the mortgage? They had recently bought a new car. One of their credit cards was at its limit. Betsy had started another job about 4 months before. Oh, and where were they going to find the money for the down payment and closing costs?

You can guess what happened. They didn't qualify for the mortgage and the deal fell apart. That's when I started to work with them. We spent the next six months getting them prepared to buy a home of their own. There are steps anyone thinking about buying a home must take. You don't want to face the disappointment that Betsy and Andrew experienced.

Yes, they finally found and bought another home. It was perfect for them. This time without the stress of wondering whether the deal will go through. Betsy and Andrew prepared this time. They also knew better than to buy their home through a listing agent.

How do you get out of renting and into a home of your own?

Do you have the resources needed to buy a home?

Is this uncertainty leaving you feeling frustrated and trapped into renting?

- Can you qualify for a mortgage?

- Is your credit good enough?

- Do you have enough money for the down payment and closing costs?

- Can you find a home you like but that you can also afford?

- Who can you trust to help you with the process?

As a result, you may be facing fear and frustration. You don't know what you don't know. As a result, you aren't sure what questions to ask or who to ask them of.

You don't want to make any mistakes.

A recent bankrate.com survey of homeowners produced some shocking results:

https://www.bankrate.com/mortgages/homebuyers-survey-february-2019/

63% of millennial homeowners surveyed regretted buying their home. 44% of all homeowners surveyed said they regretted buying their homes.

That needs repeating!

63% of millennial homeowners and 44% of all homeowners said they had buyer's remorse. They regretted buying their homes.

WOW! Let that set in for a minute.

These homebuyers wanted to take part in the American Dream of owning their own home.

They then bought the most expensive item they will ever buy.

And then, shortly after doing that, they felt buyer's remorse with the home they bought.

For these homebuyers, the American Dream turned into a nightmare.

The survey explored a little bit about why this was happening:

- Many said they weren't prepared for the actual cost of owning a home.

- Some said they bought too quick, without proper considerations.

- Others said they ended up buying a home they couldn't afford.

It is clear that people need to *"make better home buying decisions"*.

I've been a full-time real estate professional for over 45 years. I've been representing homebuyers only for the last 28 years as an exclusive buyer agent.

My real estate experience has given me a good insight into the mistakes homebuyers make. There are a lot of homebuying books out there that will educate a buyer on how to buy a home. Much of that advice is general in nature and won't vary much between authors and books.

I'm involved in two such books myself. I'm the author of the 2018 edition of "Massachusetts Homebuyers Beware! The Cards are Stacked Against You". I'm the collaborating author of the third edition of a national best-selling book. "Not One Dollar More! How to Save $3,000 to $30,000 Buying Your Next Home" by Author Joseph Cummins also was published in 2018. See "Other Books by Tom Wemett" at the end of this book.

I will be including some of this same advice here as well. But, I will also be providing you with some unique insights that you won't find in any other homebuying books.

It is my goal to help you make better homebuying decisions. This will save you money and help you to avoid costly and stupid mistakes.

How do you make better financial decisions?

Here is some good advice to start with from Allan Roth, a Financial Planner. It is from an article at aarp.org on August 8, 2016:

https://www.aarp.org/money/investing/info-2016/how-to-make-better-financial-choices-ar.html

"Take it slow when navigating your way through a maze of financial decisions. From, Nobel laureate, Daniel Kahneman's

book...Thinking, Fast and Slow. He explains that we have two systems of thinking.

System 1 is fast, instinctive, and emotional. While System 2 is slower, deliberate, and logical. Then the secret to making better financial decisions is to wait until your System 2 kicks in — or to force it to."

Steps to engage System 2, slow thinking, when making important financial decisions.

- Never make a quick decision.

Though you may convince yourself you are thinking in a logical manner, you may not be. No matter what, wait at least a day or longer. If someone tells you the offer is only good for today, run.

- Create a list of outcomes.

Make sure to write down at least a couple of ways your decision can go wrong and how much money you could lose. If you think it's a sure thing and that nothing can go wrong, then that's a strong sign System 2 hasn't engaged.

- Change roles.

Consider how the person or company selling it benefits. Their motivation may not be in your best interest.

- Get data.

How is the person different from others doing the same work? Ask questions — and demand answers.

- Discuss the decision.

Talk it over first with someone you trust and respect, but who doesn't always agree with you. This has two benefits. It forces you to try to actually understand something first. Then you can explain it to someone else. And, you are getting feedback from someone who doesn't have a vested interest in the decision.

Mr. Roth continues:

"These five steps to thinking in a slow manner, apply to all important decisions. Following them may not protect you from making mistakes in the future. But, you may make fewer and less costly mistakes."

Excellent advice when buying something as expensive as a home.

Rushing to buy a home seems to be the basic issue with those homeowners surveyed by Bankrate.com. Buying a home needs to be a serious matter to consider.

You should question whether buying a home even makes sense for you now or sometime later or ever.

I'll cover the "Renting vs. Owning" question in Chapter One.

If you do decide that you want to own your own home, you need the answers to the following questions:

Five steps to prepare for buying the right home at the right price and on the right terms.

- Do you have enough cash for a down payment and closing costs?

- Do you have credit issues or are your credit scores too low?

- Will you be able to find a home you like within your budget?

- Should you wait to be in a better purchasing position?

- Do you know who to trust and work with?

I call this the "preparation phase" of homebuying. I provide guidance for you in answering these questions in Chapters Two through Six.

After preparing to buy a home you enter what I call the "buying phase".

I cover this phase in Chapters Seven through Fourteen. This phase involves the following tasks:

- Understanding Mortgage Options and Obtaining a True Mortgage Pre-approval

- Looking at All Available Homes

- Developing a Negotiating Strategy Before Making an Offer

- Including Contingencies for Property Inspections

- Knowing What Other Contingencies to Include in Your Offer

- Continuing to Track and Follow Up

- Preparing for and Foreseeing Problems at Closing Time

- Closing and Moving-in

Buying a Home During a Pandemic

I am writing this book during the Covid-19 pandemic, an economic disaster, and a social justice crisis. You may be reading this book while these three things are still going on. I share my thoughts on this in Appendix A - Buying a Home During a Pandemic & Economic Crisis.

Resources

I have placed links to many online resources and articles thrughout the book as well as in Appendix B - Resources. These are also online at: https://make-better-homebuying-decisions.com/online-resources/

I suggest that you access these links as you read the book. That will provide an excellent basis and support for understanding the material I am presenting.

So buckle up. Let's get started on the path to YOUR homebuying success.

- I will discuss the above and more in the following pages.

- So that you can make better homebuying decisions.

- And, save money and avoid costly and stupid mistakes along the way.

Chapter One
Renting vs Owning

The title of this book suggests that "owning your own home" is better than renting.

There are a lot of financial and other advantages to owning over renting. Yet, it is wise to have a renting vs owning discussion before moving on.

If you are like some homebuyers, you may go about buying a home without giving it much thought beforehand.

Your parents may own a home. Your friends and co-workers are buying homes. So you should, too, may characterize your thinking.

But, it takes a clearer vision to make solid plans to buy a home. When I talk about vision, I'm not talking about details about the home you might like, as that comes later. This vision starts with deciding why you want to buy a home in the first place.

Whether it is your first or even if you have owned a home before, it will be the most expensive thing you will buy. It makes sense to take your time and be smart about it, before deciding to go ahead.

We covered this in the Introduction, but it is worth repeating.

Buying a home should not be an impulse buy or based on emotion. (Daniel Kahneman's Thinking System 1 - fast, instinctive, and emotional).

Rather, buying a home should be a deliberate, well-thought-out decision. It requires a specific plan of action that includes a reasonable time frame. (Daniel Kahneman's Thinking System 2 - slower, deliberate, and logical).

You need time to research the process. You need to get into the best position to buy, and then to take the right steps to ensure the best outcome.

The goal is buying the right home at the right price on the best terms.

You don't want someone selling you a home or being pushed into buying before prepared to do so.

Advantages of Renting:

Nine reasons to continue to rent and not buy a home.

- You don't have yard work or repair issues as a renter unless you are responsible for them in your lease.

- Your landlord is generally responsible for all maintenance and repair costs. These include appliances, heating, air conditioning, plumbing and electrical, roof repairs, and more.

- You don't pay homeowner's insurance or liability or flood insurance when you rent. You may have renter's insurance to cover personal liability and your personal items. Renter's insurance costs much less than homeowner's insurance.

- As a renter, you don't pay real estate taxes. Although in essence you do via the rent payment you make. But it is without the benefit of being able to deduct the cost of real estate taxes when you file your income tax.

- When you rent, you don't have the risk of a downturn in the real estate market. Such a downturn could cause you to end up with a home worth less than the mortgage you owe on it.

- You aren't tied down to one location when you rent. At the end of your lease, you are free to move. If you own a home and need or want to move, it is a far more complicated process. You have to decide what to do with the house you own.

- You may not be able to afford a home if you want to live in an urban area where the cost of buying a home could be prohibitive. Renting may be your best and only option.

- You may have access to amenities such as a pool, tennis courts or fitness center when you rent. You may not have access to these as a homeowner. Such amenities could cost you thousands of dollars more as a homeowner. A renter may have access to such amenities as part of the rent or at a reasonable extra cost.

- You don't need as much money up front to rent rather than buy a home. Even with a loan requiring a low or no down payment, you need extra cash. There are closing costs, real estate tax and insurance escrows, and moving expenses. You may also have repairs and upgrades to the home to make it your own. When renting, you need the cost of the security deposit (usually one month). You also need the first and sometimes the last month's rent, along with moving expenses, and you can move in.

I recommend David Bach's best-selling book, "The Automatic Millionaire Homeowner".

He believes that buying a home is an investment that everyone can enjoy benefits from. Not prioritizing homeownership is:

"the single biggest mistake millennials are making. If millennials don't buy a home, their chances of actually having any wealth in this country are little to none."

"As a renter, you can spend half a million dollars or more on rent over the years. ($1,500 a month for 30 years comes to $540,000) And, in the end wind up where you started—owning nothing. Or you can buy a house and spend the same amount paying down a mortgage. In the end you wind up owning your own home free and clear!"

The Net Worth of a Homeowner is 44x Greater Than A Renter!

As reported at keepcurrentmatters.com.
https://www.keepingcurrentmatters.com/2018/08/20/the-net-worth-of-a-homeowner-is-44x-greater-than-a-renter/

"Every three years, the Federal Reserve conducts their Survey of Consumer Finances in which they collect data across all economic and social groups. Their latest survey data, covering 2013-2016 was recently released.

The study revealed that the median net worth of a homeowner was $231,400 – a 15% increase since 2013. At the same time, the median net worth of renters decreased by 5% ($5,200 today compared to $5,500 in 2013). These numbers reveal that the net worth of a homeowner is over 44 times greater than that of a renter."

Advantages of Homeownership:

Five reasons why owning your own home makes more sense than renting.

- Tax Advantages. Mortgage interest and real estate taxes may be deductible on your income tax return. But, the tax deduction may or may not be helpful for you depending on your income tax situation. If you don't itemize but take the standard deduction, then there might not be any tax advantages. The amount of the deductions might not be greater than the standard deduction. If you already itemize deductions then you will be able to reap extra tax advantages. Talk to a professional tax adviser to review your financial situation. They will tell you what advantage, if any, owning a home might make in your annual tax situation.

- Forced Savings. You pay your rent on-time to avoid an eviction from your apartment. You will do whatever it takes to pay your mortgage on time as well to avoid a foreclosure and losing your home. The difference is that you will be building equity in your home each month. Part of each mortgage payment is a principal payment. This reduces the amount that you owe. That increases the equity in the home. Equity is the difference between the value of your home and the balance you owe on the mortgage.

- Building Asset Value. There are two more ways that you may increase your equity in your home. The first is "forced appreciation" by means of improvements you make to the home. You force the increase in value and equity you have in the home by means of improving the property and its value. The actual value added by means of your direct labor is often referred to as "sweat equity." Improvements that actually upgrade the property should result in an increase in value. The second is "market appreciation" when the market for real estate is increasing. The increasing market should also increase the value of your home as well. The real estate market goes in cycles, up and down. We recently saw the market drop in 2007 and 2008. But in most real estate markets across the country, prices have rebounded. In some urban areas buyers are paying prices that exceed asking prices by ten or twenty percent or more.

- Pride of Ownership. Most people take pride in their home whether renting or owning. Any repairs or improvements you make to an apartment may benefit you while you live there. But they benefit the landlord more than they do you. By owning a home, you in essence become your own landlord. Any repairs, replacements or improvements benefit you.

- Personal Freedoms. By owning your own home, you have some freedoms that you don't have right now while renting. How about planting a garden? We have a garden and enjoy having our own vegetables to eat. There is a unique enjoyment of tending our own garden. A lot of work but very rewarding. How about having a private yard for your children or pets to play in? We have a dog that loves to play in the yard. We also have three beehives and bottle our own honey which we give to friends and relatives. How about having a nice patio with your own barbeque grill and private area for relaxing and hanging out? What a wonderful feeling having friends or neighbors over for a cookout. What about room for an above-ground pool? I'm not crazy about having a pool. Are you and your family? What about room to park a second car, boat, or RV? Skip the parking restrictions or extra charge to park your extra vehicle, boat, or RV.

Buying Now or Waiting:

- So, what is your vision of owning your own home?

- What is your reason if your decision is to buy a home?

- Have you taken into consideration renting vs owning?

- Are you making a deliberate rather than emotional decision to buy a home?

- Are you willing to be patient if things don't quite work out for you right now? Are you in a financial position to buy a home today, or do you need to wait a while? You may need to wait a few months or a year or more.

- Do you have enough money saved currently? Can you take on the financial responsibility of buying a home right now?

- If your employment is questionable, you may want to wait a while to make sure your income source is stable.

- Are you considering a new job? It would be best to wait until you are in the new job for a while to make sure you are comfortable in your new surroundings. If you are changing careers, it may be difficult to get a mortgage unless you have a track record in your line of work. A potential lender may want to wait to see how your work situation develops.

- Are you due a raise in pay or a bonus such that waiting a while might make buying a home less stressful?

- Are you due a large income tax refund that you want to use to buy a home with?

- Do you have credit issues that may need time and effort to correct and improve?

- Are you in a lease that doesn't expire for another year. Does it have a provision to leave early or cancel the lease? Will it cost you a lot of money or will you lose your security deposit?

- Do you need to spend some time taking a look at your spending and savings habits? You might be able to make some adjustments to pay off or pay down debt. You might be able to build up a savings fund and an emergency fund. You may feel more comfortable taking on a mortgage. Such an action plan might be the first step in preparing to buy a home.

So, you have a choice.

You can continue wondering and dreaming about owning your own home and take no action. Or, you can take steps today to explore the idea of owning your own home and what it will take to do so.

You don't know what you don't know.

- What questions should you be asking?

- What steps should you be taking?

- What pitfalls and challenges will you encounter?

- Who can you trust to help you and be your guide?

I will answer these questions and more for you throughout the rest of this book.

So, are you ready to begin to explore becoming a proud, happy homeowner?

You are the HERO of the story that is about to unfold.

Are You a Homebuying Hero? "A person admired for achievements and noble qualities and who shows great courage". This meets my definition of a Hero.

Not everyone is willing to take the time and effort to understand what it takes to buy a home. Remember our discussion of Thinking, Fast and Slow and the two systems of thinking. System 1 is fast, instinctive, and emotional. While System 2 is slower, deliberate, and logical.

A true Homebuying Hero will focus on System 2. They will go slower and make deliberate and logical decisions. These will be better homebuying decisions. Those homebuyers who make fast, instinctive and emotional decisions are the ones who end up with buyer's remorse. They end up a statistic in the Bankrate.com survey.

The definition of a Hero showing great courage describes those who do take the steps and the time to learn. They make a specific plan to buy their own home. They are willing to sacrifice some non-essentials currently. The long term goal is to own their own home.

Think of how you will feel achieving that goal. But, also think about how others will see you as a new homeowner. Envious? Impressed? Admired?

Yes, you as the Homebuying Hero "a person admired for achievements and noble qualities".

Hard to imagine yourself as a Hero?

Any story involving a Hero usual involves someone who also doesn't think of themselves as a Hero. But they evolve into one as the story progresses.

Afraid of the obstacles? Fearful of the process? You should be. There is a lot to buying a home. But as any Hero discovers, a Guide usually appears to help the Hero out.

Consider myself and this book your Guide. Follow the steps. Become a smart homebuyer. Ask for further help when you feel you need it. My contact information is at the beginning of this book on the copyright page. Feel free to contact me to discuss any questions you might have about homebuying.

Remember, you are the Hero in the story that will unfold as we go through the homebuying process.

You want to stop renting and own a home of your own, right?

You may be feeling some frustration and fear. Yet, you prepare yourself and your family to becoming proud, happy homeowners.

To help you keep your focus, try visualizing living in a home of your own.

Picture yourself and your family moving into your own home. Put together a story board with pictures. Involve your children. Ask them to draw a picture of the home they would like to live in. Involve them in the process. One of my client's son drew a picture of a home that even included an area he labeled, "man cave". Moving is especially difficult for children. Involve them in the process in meaningful ways.

- What do you see?

- How are you feeling?

- Write down your feelings. Doesn't need to be anything fancy, one word or two-or-three-word phrases are good enough.

- Do you feel a sense of pride at becoming a homeowner at last?

- Do you see yourself setting up a garden?

- How about the swing set and play area for the kids?

- Is there a fenced-in area where your dog can run and play?

Now is the time to start exploring these feelings.

You will need to reach back and bring forth those feelings again as you go through the process. There are pitfalls. There are setbacks. This is going to be an adventure and occasional challenge.

In the next several chapters we will explore the steps necessary to buy a home of your own. Through this process you will get a better understanding of what it takes to own a home of your own. You will discover if homeownership is a worthwhile goal for yourself and your family.

Preparation is the key to successful homebuying.

If done right, you won't experience the buyer's remorse many of your peers have experienced. You are smarter than that!

Chapter Two
Do You Have Enough Cash
for a Down Payment & Closing Costs?

From a recent report from the Urban Institute.

"Barriers to Accessing Homeownership - Down Payment, Credit, and Affordability – September 2018".

https://www.urban.org/research/publication/barriers-accessing-homeownership-down-payment-credit-and-affordability-2018
(Click on the button to the right to download the 32 page *"pdf"* file.)

"Saving for a down payment is a considerable barrier to homeownership. Renters see the inability to save for a down payment as one of the leading obstacles. Many renters surveyed indicated they could not afford a down payment. As such they continue to rent."

"Most consumers are unfamiliar with low–down payment programs. Most homebuyers are unaware there are low and no down payment programs available. There are programs available at the local, state, and federal levels. These can help eligible borrowers secure an appropriate down payment."

Only 19% of consumers believe lenders would make loans with a down payment of 5% or less. While close to 40% of consumers do not know what to expect.

You don't need 20% down. The national median down payment is 7%. Some mortgage programs only need a 3.5% down payment such as FHA, and some need no money down such as VA and USDA.

Keep in mind there are other closing costs as well you need cash for. These could equal another 4% to 6% of the price you pay. That would be between $8,000 and $12,000 for a $200,000 home.

There are many ways that you can come up with cash for a down payment and closing costs.

Take a look at your spending.

In fact, that should be the first thing you do before even considering buying a home.

You need to sit down and analyze your spending habits. List your net income from all sources. List your expenses. What expenses are necessary? These include rent, credit card payments, student loan payments, car payments, food, etc.

If you lack cash for a down payment and closing costs can you make adjustments to these expenses? For example, cut down on food cost by not eating out as often. Cut back on unnecessary purchases. These include clothing that satisfies a desire to have the latest fashion.

Where can you cut back? Revisit the vision we talked about in the previous chapter. This should be the inspiration to make these choices.

Can you find a way to make more income?

Can you take a part time job or start a part time business? An extra $300 to $500 a month will make a big difference.

Are you saving money for an emergency fund?

Experts suggest you should have between 3 and 6 months of income set aside for emergencies. Having such a fund will give you peace of mind to take on a mortgage and the expenses of owning your own home.

Here are some more suggestions:

Ten ways to find cash for your down payment and closing costs.

- Income-tax refund.

- Loan against the cash value of life insurance policies.

- Selling a car, boat, trailer, or other asset.

- Getting married? Instead of people giving you toasters ask them to give you cash to help with buying a home.

- Gift from a relative: Do you have any relatives who could loan you money or are willing to make a gift to you of money to help out? You never know. Let your relatives know that you are contemplating buying a home, and one of them may be willing to help.

Most loan programs allow gifts from family members. These can assist a buyer with down payments and/or closing costs. These programs do restrict the amount of the gift.

If a relative is willing to make a gift to you of money, the relative will have to sign a bank document. This certifies that the money is not a loan but rather a gift. Lenders generally do not allow loans from other sources for the down payment. The exception being loans from your retirement accounts as these funds are your own.

What if a relative is willing to give you money but expects you to pay it back? The money needs to be in your bank account for 60 to 90 days before submitting a mortgage application. As long as the money has time for "seasoning" to happen, such documentation isn't needed. A bank wants copies of your last two to three months of statements. They won't need an explanation for deposits in prior months. You and your relative can make arrangements to pay them back upon agreed-upon terms.

- Are you a valuable employee with a smaller company? See if the company will contribute money toward buying your home. I had a client, George, who was a valuable employee with his company. George mentioned he planned to buy a home. His company gave him an immediate bonus of five thousand dollars. My client had to pay taxes on the bonus. But after taxes, it remained a nice surprise and helped out in his being able to find the right home.

- Do you qualify for special down payment or closing cost programs? I have a link to a website to find down payment resources nationally. www.down-payment-finder.com This website provides information on such programs. You enter a city, state, specific address, or zip code to see what programs are available. You can then determine if you are eligible.

- Lender Closing Cost Help: Lenders can also help with a closing cost credit. The lender will increase the interest rate to offset the credit. But it still may make sense to go this route as well. Discuss this with your mortgage specialist.

- Seller Closing Cost Help: The seller can help pay for the closing costs. Most mortgage programs allow this "seller concession". A seller can contribute between 3% and 6% of the price of the home toward the buyer's closing costs.

It is a matter of negotiation between the buyer and the seller depending on the buyer's needs. The seller will generally ask for a higher price to offset the closing cost credit. So it may be the buyer who ends up paying for the credit in most cases. Yet, that still might be worthwhile to allow you to buy sooner rather than later.

A quick comment on seller concessions. Yes, the seller can take some of the price you pay and give it back to you to help with your closing costs. But when the seller looks at their bottom line, the net cash received, they may want to increase the price you pay. This is to cover the amount you are asking to have returned to you for closing costs.

So, for example if you offered $200,000 and wanted $6,000 back from the seller the seller would net $194,000. If the seller wanted $200,000 net of seller concessions they will counter with a price of $206,000. They would give you back $6,000 and net themselves the $200,000.

You may have added $6,000 to the price you are paying and to your mortgage and you will be paying it back over 30 years. Keep that in mind. There may be better methods than using a seller concession. One such method is borrowing against a retirement account discussed next.

- Borrowing against a retirement account such as a 401k or IRA, is one of the best ways to get more money. These retirement plans generally allow a loan against the account for buying a home. If used to buy a home you won't incur an income tax penalty. As this is a loan from your own money and you pay it back to yourself it isn't considered a taxable event.

When compared to getting money from a seller concession, this is better. Instead of paying back the amount plus interest to a bank over 30 years you are paying it back to yourself. This is over a much shorter period and you are paying interest to yourself.

Many financial planners will argue against borrowing against a retirement account. This is due to the fear that you may not pay it back or that you will use the money for something frivolous. I can't think of a better way to use such money then helping you buy an asset that generally increases in value over time. And, that helps you build more equity.

Besides, as noted above, it is your money that you now pay back to yourself with interest. So your retirement account isn't harmed in the long term.

Should you wait to put 20% down?

Some will argue that putting 20% down is more prudent. 20% or more down provides a safety net by way of having more equity in your home. The difference between the value of your home and the mortgage balance is the equity you have in your home. In the event of a downturn in the economy or need to sell, you have more cushion. In 2008 there was a huge economic downturn that caused a lot of homeowners to lose their homes. As prices dropped, those without equity often had no other course but foreclosure.

Another factor in favor of a down payment of 20% or more is to avoid PMI, Private Mortgage Insurance. If you are getting an FHA mortgage it is MIP, Mortgage Insurance Premium. Banks are reluctant to lend money with less than 20% down.

To get lenders to consider lower down payments the lenders want an insurance policy. This protects them in the event of a foreclosure. This is an extra upfront and/or monthly payment made with your regular mortgage payment.

If you are putting less than 20% down on a conventional loan once the equity in your home reaches 22% the PMI drops. The equity is the original home appraisal price less the balance of the mortgage.

But, in the meantime, your monthly mortgage payment could be $100 or more higher, than it would have been with 20% down to begin with.

Over time home prices generally continue to go up. So waiting until you have saved up a 20% down payment may result in your paying a higher price. That could offsets the idea of waiting.

Your personal financial situation will determine if waiting to buy makes sense. Or, if buying now using a low or no down payment loan program makes sense.

Some real-life examples:

For one of my buyer clients.

Jim was able to negotiate a credit from the seller at closing for $6,000. Jim used this toward his closing costs. Also, his down payment on a $100,000 home was 3.5% - $3,500. His total out of pocket was around $4,500.

For another recent buyer client.

Joe was able to buy a home with no down payment through a USDA loan. This is a loan program available through the US Department of Agriculture. It is available in most rural areas around the country. Joe and his wife purchased a $200,000 home with no down payment. They also got some closing cost help from the seller. Their out of pocket costs were around $3,000.

Another consideration:

Seasoning Cash Deposits:

I mentioned this above. Make sure that you don't stick a bunch of cash into your account that you can't document. Some people save up cash but don't place it in an account until they are ready to buy a home. You may have some cash from working "under the table" or selling some items on eBay or in a yard sale. Or you may have tip money that wasn't deposited anywhere. These are hard to document.

Such cash has to be "seasoned". It must be in your bank account at least for between sixty and ninety days before applying for a mortgage. Otherwise you will need to prove the source of any recent cash deposits. It is easy to document your regular pay checks but impossible to document the items above.

Chapter Three
Do You Have Credit Issues
or are Your Credit Scores Too Low?

More from the Urban Institute report:

https://www.urban.org/research/publication/barriers-accessing-homeownership-down-payment-credit-and-affordability-2018

"Access to homeownership is not limited by down payments alone. Credit access is tight by historical standards. The median credit score of new mortgage originations has increased in the post-crisis-period. The median credit score for mortgages is 779, compared with the pre-crisis median of 692. Credit scores of FHA borrowers have been lower; the current median credit score is 671."

Check you credit reports early.

Homebuyers often wait until they have a property under contract. Or, until they apply for a mortgage. If errors or problems arise, great delays and heartaches can result.

It can take five months to get inaccurate information removed from credit reports. Even longer for credit scores to readjust and increase. This would delay qualifying for a mortgage or for a reduced interest rate.

In the meantime, if you have a home under contract, the seller isn't going to want to wait. And, you may have already spent money on inspections. And you still haven't bought a home.

Sloppy Credit Bureau Practices:

From the USPIRG, US Public Interest Research Group:

https://uspirg.org/news/usf/new-report-analyzes-complaints-about-credit-bureaus

"The most valuable thing we have is our good name. As consumers, the most common reflection of our reputation as someone who pays bills on time, is trustworthy and financially sound is our credit report. Unfortunately, the information contained in our credit reports, which are bought and sold daily to nearly anyone who requests and pays for them, does not always tell a true story."

Credit bureaus collect and compile information about consumer creditworthiness from banks and other creditors and from public record sources such as lawsuits, tax liens and legal judgements. The three major credit bureaus -- Experian (formerly TRW), Equifax, and Trans Union -- maintain files on nearly 90 percent of all American adults. Those files are routinely sold to credit grantors, landlords, employers, insurance companies, and many others interested in the credit record of a consumer, often (legally) without the consumer's knowledge or permission.

Conversely, consumers rarely check their credit record until after they've been denied or otherwise encountered a problem. Throughout the 1990s, credit report errors have been a serious problem that several states and Congress have addressed.

This is the PIRGs' sixth study on credit report accuracy and privacy issues since 1991.

The PIRGs have also participated in state and federal legislative battles to improve credit reporting laws. This report is our first investigation of credit report accuracy since 1996 Congressional changes to the federal Fair Credit Reporting Act (FCRA), designed to improve the accuracy and ease of access to reports, took effect in September 1997.

The findings of the survey, Mistakes Can Happen, are troubling.

*An alarming number of credit reports contain serious errors
that could cause the denial of credit, a loan, or even a job.
Further, some consumers never even received their reports,
even after repeated calls.*

Among the major credit report accuracy findings of the survey:

- Twenty-nine percent (29%) of the credit reports contained serious errors.

*These false delinquencies or accounts that did not belong to the
consumer often resulted in the denial of credit.*

- Forty-one percent (41%) of the credit reports contained inaccurate personal demographic identifying information.

*The information was misspelled, long-outdated, belonged to a
stranger, or was otherwise incorrect.*

- Twenty percent (20%) of the credit reports had missing accounts.

*These major credit, loan, mortgage, or other consumer
accounts often demonstrated the creditworthiness of the
consumer.*

- Twenty-six percent (26%) of the credit reports contained mis-identified items.

*There were credit accounts that had been closed by the
consumer but incorrectly remained listed as open.*

- Altogether, 70% of the credit reports contained either serious errors or other mistakes of some kind.

Among the survey's major access to credit report findings:

- Of the consumers that did obtain their credit reports, at least 14% of them were forced to call back 3 or more times after receiving busy signals or had to write a letter in order to receive their report.

- And 12% of the consumers waited two weeks or longer to receive their report once they finished requesting it. It took more than a month for one California man to receive his report.

- Overall, 15% of consumers who attempted to participate in the survey either made at least 3 phone calls and never got through or requested their reports but never received them.

Although credit reports contain vitally important information about most consumers, the accuracy of those reports is far from guaranteed. Further information from the USPIRG.

https://uspirgedfund.org/reports/usf/big-credit-bureaus-big-mistakes

While credit bureaus and creditors have gone to great lengths to ensure that they have the right to collect and compile monstrous lists of information about most of us, mistakes in credit reports do happen, and more often than credit bureaus and, also, banks and department stores (who are often responsible for the mistakes) would like us to think. Until policymakers and credit bureaus do what it takes to allow consumers to have free and easy access to their credit reports and set tougher standards to prevent and clean-up mistakes, too many credit reports will remain a ticking timebomb of dangerously inaccurate information.

And our good names will continue to be at risk, as we pay the price for mistakes made by credit bureaus and other data dealers.

From a 2012 Federal Trade Commission study mandated by Congress.

https://www.ftc.gov/news-events/press-releases/2015/01/ftc-issues-follow-study-credit-report-accuracy

"One in five consumers has an error in at least one of three major credit reports."

The Federal Trade Commission has issued a follow-up study of credit report accuracy that found most consumers who previously reported an unresolved error on one of their three major credit reports believe that at least one piece of disputed information on their report is still inaccurate.

The congressionally mandated study is the sixth and final study on national credit report accuracy by the FTC. It follows up on a study issued by the FTC in 2012, which examined how many consumers had errors on one of their three major credit reports.

The 2012 study found, among other things, that one in five consumers had an error that was corrected by a credit reporting agency (CRA) after it was disputed on at least one of their three credit reports. The study also found that about 20 percent of consumers who identified errors on one of their three major credit reports experienced an increase in their credit score that resulted in a decrease in their credit risk tier, making them more likely to be offered a lower auto loan interest rate.

A high percentage of credit reports contain mistakes of some kind.

So have I made my point?

Do you agree? It makes sense to check your credit early in the process!

Most lenders use the FICO credit score as the main basis for a mortgage.

This is a number based on a formula developed by the Fair Isaac Corporation. Fair Isaac is an analytics software company. They provide industry-acknowledged summaries of credit accounts and payment history.

Your FICO credit score will determine your access to and cost of credit. The higher the FICO score, the better, and the lower, the more problems.

FICO scores range from 300-850. Fair Isaac calculates them for each of the three big credit-reporting agencies. These are: TransUnion, Equifax, and Experian.

Lenders generally use the middle FICO score to determine credit worthiness.

They often work from a grid showing credit score ranges and down payment percentages. They use this to determine the interest rate for a loan. They also use this to determine the amount of points you need to pay to get a better interest rate. So paying attention to your credit and credit scores could pay off long-term.

For more information about credit reporting and credit scores go to the MyFico.com website.

https://www.myfico.com/credit-education

Determining a FICO Score:

- Thirty-five percent determined by payment history. Do you pay bills on time to any creditor that submits information to the credit bureau? Overdue medical bills, utility bills, and other bills can cause a problem.

- Thirty percent based on amounts owed to each of your creditors compared to the total credit line. If you're maxing out credit cards, your score may suffer. It appears that the ideal is keep balances below thirty percent of the credit line.

- Fifteen percent determined by the length of credit history. This considers both the age of each account and how recent any activity. The fewer and older the accounts, the better.

- Ten percent based on how many recently opened accounts out of the total number of accounts. The number of recent inquiries made by lenders also matters. Your score can drop if it looks as if you're seeking several new sources of credit. This could be a sign that you may be in financial trouble.

Lender inquiries about your credit without your knowledge should not affect your score. An example is with credit offers.

Shopping around for a mortgage shouldn't hurt, either, if you search within a six-week period or less.

Each inquiry for a credit card could reduce your credit scores, so be selective.

- Ten percent involves the types of credit used. Installment debt with a fixed amount each month indicates the ability to manage a large loan. How a debtor handles revolving debt is more predictive of future behavior. This includes how you pay your credit cards.

Do you pay off the balance each month or the least that is due, for example? Do you charge to the limit of cards or rarely use them?

Five ways to screw up your mortgage and home purchase:

- You shouldn't take on new credit or apply for credit in the months leading to the decision to buy a home. This pertains especially during the time you have a home under contract.

I've had buyers buy a new car while their mortgage application was under process. The new loan came to the attention of the mortgage company. The buyers didn't qualify for the mortgage due to higher debt-to-income ratios. Because they didn't qualify for enough credit and had no other resources the buyers lost the home.

Buyers may also end up losing a deposit if they are no longer qualified for a loan. If the period of loan contingency expired, they can't get their deposit back.. Mortgage companies request a credit report before closing a loan. They do this to see if the buyers have taken out new loans since the original credit report. If they have, they might not qualify for a loan as noted above.

- You shouldn't co-sign loans for anyone. It doesn't matter if the payments made on those loans are by someone else. Because your name is on them, they still count against your debt-to-income ratios. This could cause problems with an approval for a mortgage.

- You shouldn't change banks during or before applying for a mortgage. The lender may want an account at the lending institution. This may help to get a loan or better interest rate. Keep the existing account open until after the loan closes.

- You shouldn't close credit accounts. Closing accounts could lower your credit scores especially if they are older accounts. Part of the credit score calculation is the age of your accounts. So closing an older account will cause the average age to rise and thus the potential to lower your score.

- You shouldn't pay off old debt and collections. This often causes your credit scores to go down. Paying them off may trigger a new seven-year period. Negative items can remain on a report for seven years before credit bureaus remove the item.

You or someone on your behalf should first attempt to negotiate a pay for deletion agreement. The collection agency or creditor deletes the item from your credit report if you pay in full or at a discount.

But, your lender may want certain outstanding debts paid off at closing. You should discuss whether to pay off outstanding debts with your lender.

Why do mortgage lenders pay so much attention to FICO scores?

Statistics provide lenders with guidance. A borrower with a FICO score below six hundred has a one in eight chance they will be delinquent or default on a loan. A borrower with a score above eight hundred has a one in thirteen hundred chance of similar problems. Thus, lenders rely on credit score evaluation systems.

So what can you do to get and keep a higher score?

Three ways to get and keep a higher credit score.

- First, make your payments on time.

- Second, refrain from applying for new credit.

- Third, do not use more than 30% of your credit limits.

Where do you get your own credit reports and credit scores?

There are many credit reporting agencies. But lenders tend to rely on three major US credit bureaus. These are: Equifax, Experian, and TransUnion:

Equifax: https://www.equifax.com/personal/

Experian: https://www.experian.com/

TransUnion: https://www.transunion.com/

Mortgage companies get a "tri-merge" credit report from all three credit reporting agencies. It includes your FICO credit scores from all three as well. Most lenders will do this at no cost to the borrower as part of a mortgage pre-qualification. This is less expensive than buying your credit reports and scores from all three bureaus.

But, the lender may only pull a soft pull or only from one credit bureau. Ask the lender to see if they will pull a tri-merge from all three. You need to know what all three FICO credit scores are. You need to know where to focus your attention.

You can get your credit reports for free and pay for your credit scores yourself.

The Fair and Accurate Credit Transactions Act of 2003—the FACT Act. This requires credit bureaus to provide one free credit report every twelve months. The official web site is:

https://www.annualcreditreport.com/index.action.

A special alert from the above website: *"During these times of COVID-19, accessing your credit is important. That's why Equifax, Experian, and TransUnion are now offering free weekly online reports through April 2021."*

I also noticed that each of the three credit bureaus may be offering free credit scores along with credit reports on their respective websites due to the above concern during the Covid-19 pandemic.

I suggest that you access the annualcreditreport.com website from a desktop computer connected to a printer so that you can print out your credit report. You have the option of downloading it and printing it later or printing it as you are on the site.

More information is available on the Federal Trade Commission's web site – https://www.ftc.gov/.

Click on the Get Your Free Credit Report button on the right side.

The free report doesn't include your credit score. Each credit bureau will charge extra for your credit score. Thus getting your credit scores from a lender when you get pre-qualified at no cost may make more sense.

Caution: Some credit scores offered by the credit bureaus and others are consumer scores.

These are not identical to what a lender requires or uses and are deceptive.

The Consumer Financial Protection Bureau recently took action against Experian and its subsidiaries. They were deceiving consumers about the use of credit scores it sold to consumers.

Experian claimed lenders used their credit scores to make credit decisions. But lenders didn't use Experian's scores for that purpose.

The Consumer Financial Protection Bureau, CFPB, is a US government agency. They oversee banks, lenders, and other financial companies. The CFPB is an excellent source of information about credit and homebuying.

Navigate to the CFPB consumer website - https://www.consumerfinance.gov/.

Then check under Consumer Tools (located in the top menu on the far left) for more information about financial related subjects. There are additional tools and resources under, "Buying a Home".

You can buy all three credit reports and FICO scores at:

https://www.myfico.com/products/fico-score-credit-reports/.

For a one-time fee of sixty dollars you get all three credit reports and FICO scores. This is a good option if you decide to check your credit and credit scores early on your own. Before you do this check with each credit bureau to see if they are providing their FICO score for free due to the pandemic.

Challenging Credit Report Errors:

Married couples should get individual reports rather than joint reports.

It is easier to challenge inaccurate information person by person. It is easier to challenge information on reports obtained from each credit bureau. It is harder to challenge information from a combination report. Challenges must be sent to each individual credit bureau.

Reports obtained at www.annualcreditreport.com are separate. These are easier to review and then, if necessary, challenge inaccurate information.

Even if you got a combined tri-merge report from a lender you may want to get your individual reports. This will make challenging issues easier to do.

You may want to start with the original vendor/creditor for inaccurate items.

Do this before filing a challenge with the credit reporting agencies. Many medical collections are the result of improper filing with insurance companies. Contact the doctor or hospital and ask them about the item.

If information is inaccurate or items aren't yours, follow the next steps:

- Review reports and note inaccurate or unknown information. I recommend circling inaccurate items and noting what is wrong with the item. State things such as: "*not mine*"; "*unknown*"; or "*not accurate*" as the case may be.

- Then mail a hard copy of the report to the relevant reporting agencies. Ask for *validation* of inaccurate items. Most people ask a credit bureau for *verification* rather than validation. It is easier for credit bureaus to meet the legal threshold for *verification*. The law requires validation, so ask for *validation*.

- Send the original report with the notations on it via USPS Priority Mail. That way you have a receipt and record of when it arrived at the credit bureau. Keep a copy of the report before you mail it.

- Go online to www.USPS.com and enter your tracking number. Then print out the notice that indicates the delivery date. That way you have proof of delivery.

- Credit bureaus have a thirty to forty-five-day window for reviewing questioned items. They should reply about what they found and what action(s) they will take. They have the options of removing or correcting the entry.

- Some situations may need several attempts to get an accurate report from each agency.

- Credit reporting agencies are good at delay. If you want to have inaccuracies removed from your credit report, keep at it. Stick to your guns.

What about negative information, such as bankruptcy, judgments, and collections?

Credit reporting agencies must remove bankruptcies from your credit report after ten years. They must remove judgments, collections, and other negative items after seven years. This is from the date of last activity.

Yet, nothing in the law requires any negative item to remain for a specific time. Many people with negative items believe they are in a figurative credit prison. This could last for from seven to ten years.

If credit bureaus report inaccurate information within an item, you can challenge it. Ask for validation of the item. If they can't provide validation of the item they should remove it. Or, if they can't correct inaccurate information, they should remove the item.

The credit bureaus decided to remove new and existing tax-lien and civil-judgment data. This started on July 1, 2017. The credit bureaus will do so if the data doesn't include a list of at least three data points to insure accuracy. This would include a person's name; address; and either a social security number or date of birth.

Many liens and most judgments don't include all three or four. Often bankruptcy records don't show accurate information either.

Can I qualify for a mortgage if I have a recent bankruptcy or home foreclosure?

Yes, provided you meet certain requirements. There are variations of these requirements. Check with a mortgage professional to discuss you specific situation.

Start by checking your credit reports to make sure that any discharged debt is listed as "included in bankruptcy". If it remains open rather than showing this status, it will hurt your credit score.

FHA mortgages have the most lenient requirements for qualifying following a bankruptcy or home foreclosure. Here is a brief summary of these requirements.

For a Chapter 7, straight bankruptcy where you have received a discharge, you need to wait a minimum of two years. This requirement could be longer depending on how you have managed your finances since your discharge.

- Have you reestablished credit?

- Have you made all payments on time?

- Is your employment stable?

- Are your financial problems you had previously now under control?

For a Chapter 13, where you are making payments over a three to five year period, you may be able to qualify immediately without a wait. You must be making your Chapter 13 payments to the court on time. The bankruptcy trustee for your case, however, must approve the home purchase. The trustee has to feel comfortable that you can handle a home purchase as well as the monthly payments to creditors.

For foreclosures, short-sales or deed-in-lieu of foreclosures, the waiting period for FHA loans is three years. Depending on the circumstances that was the cause of one of these, FHA might consider a shorter time. A mortgage underwriter will want to see evidence of financial stability. In general, underwriters look for:

- Did you have good credit before the event?

- Have you reestablished good credit since the event?

- Was the event caused by a one-time event?

- Are you now recovered or have you made fundamental changes in your life since the event?

What about credit repair companies?

Getting inaccurate information removed from your credit reports will take time and patience. But, there is no reason to hire a credit repair company to do it for you.

They are expensive to use and often not worth the cost. They will do the same things and follow the same procedures that you can on your own but charge you for it.

The Consumer Financial Protection Bureau issued a warning. *"How to tell a reputable credit counselor from a bogus credit repair company."*

"There are counselors who can help you with your credit report, and others who take your money but don't help you. Warning signs include companies that ask you to pay before providing services. The company may claim that it can guarantee a specific increase in your credit score. Or get rid of negative credit information in your credit report. This is even though the information is accurate and current."

More information is at: https://www.consumerfinance.gov/ask-cfpb/how-can-i-tell-a-credit-repair-scam-from-a-reputable-credit-counselor-en-1343/

The article includes a link to a list of legitimate, approved credit counselors. They provide some added advice.

- Develop a list of potential counseling agencies.

- Check them out with your State Attorney General's office.

- Check with a local consumer protection agency.

- Ask the credit counseling agency for free information about their services. Ask for details on what they provide. A reputable credit counseling agency should be willing to send you free information. It should include information about itself and the services it provides. They should do this without requiring you to provide details about your situation. If a service doesn't do that, consider it a red flag, and go elsewhere for help".

Also, if you are in touch with a lender, ask your lender to help you with the process.

- They have had other clients with such challenges.

- They should be able to provide advice and help in your case.

- Lenders sometimes have an expedited method to process direct to credit bureaus. This can speed up the process when there are obvious errors, so ask if your potential lender can help.

Beware that not all lenders want to or can help you.

If you have credit issues many lenders will dismiss you and tell you to come back when your credit is better.

Remember Jim from above?

Jim, rather than having horrible credit, had no credit. As a result he had no credit score and couldn't qualify for a mortgage. Jim had met with other mortgage representatives. One of them was at his bank where he had his account. One by one they all told him they couldn't help him and to come back when he had built up some credit.

Not one offered suggestions or gave Jim any guidance about what to do. Jim thought he was at a dead end and that his dream of owning his own home was going up in a puff of smoke. But Jim persisted as he wanted his own place and he refused to give up.

A lender I referred Jim to suggested that Jim get a secured credit card. Jim put $200 dollars in a savings account with the credit card company. Then the limit on the card was the $200 he had in the savings account. Jim used the card every month to pay bills and then paid it off in full each month.

Three months later, Jim's credit score was enough to qualify for a mortgage. Today Jim and his family are living in their own home.

Most credit issues, including judgements, bankruptcies, and foreclosures, need time to fix.

A proper plan is needed to put yourself back into a position to qualify for a mortgage.

Another of my buyer clients had success in improving her credit as well.

Mary was a single mom raising two kids. Mary had a good job but horrible credit. Mary and her children lived in an apartment complex that offered no privacy. Mary knew she had to find a home of her own, so she could provide a better environment for her young children.

The apartment was in a rough part of town and she often feared for the safety of her children and herself. She didn't want her children playing outside alone. She also knew that moving to a better apartment would cost her more than she could afford.

Mary was willing to do whatever it would take to get out of that apartment complex. She wanted to provide a safe secure home of her own for herself and her children.

We started by pulling her credit reports and seeing where she was at. As I said, Mary's credit was horrible. There were collections, write-offs, judgments, and a bunch of stuff that wasn't even hers. The situation looked hopeless.

Yet, Mary and I worked out a plan of attack and met every month for 14 months. Mary sent letters and challenged errors with my help and guidance. I also helped her to negotiate a couple of payoff agreements. This is where Mary paid a discounted amount for a collection item. This was in exchange for removing the collection item from Mary's credit reports.

The process took time. It took a lot of work and perseverance. But Mary succeeded.

Credit bureaus are notorious for using delaying tactics. But I had been through this before with other clients. Mary thought she was never going to be able to buy a home. But, her persistence and focus on the goal of owning her own home paid off. After working on improving her credit she was finally able to qualify for a mortgage. She was able to buy the perfect home for herself and her family.

Need help with improving your credit?

Have questions about credit or credit scoring? Contact a legitimate credit counseling organization as noted above. Make a plan, and stick to it. You will be successful as well in owning your own home like Jim and Mary were able to do. If you have any questions feel free to email me: tom@tomwemett.com.

Chapter Four
Will You be Able to Find a Home You Like Within Your Budget?

Some further content from the Urban Institute's report:

https://www.urban.org/research/publication/barriers-accessing-homeownership-down-payment-credit-and-affordability-2018

"Because of the increase in home prices, national home price affordability has declined. Low interest rates have aided affordability. Lower down payments help with buying a home, but they increase monthly payments."

We discussed renting vs. owning in Chapter One and the advantages of one over the other. This chapter will help you decide if you can afford to buy a home that meets your needs in the area in which you want to live.

Owning a home with a mortgage is more affordable than renting in most parts of the country.

On a national level, a median income family spends 28 percent of its income to pay rent. But spends only 25 percent of its income to afford the monthly mortgage payment with 3.5 percent down.

So, what is affordability in the state in which you live or where you want to buy a home? And, is it more affordable to rent or to buy there?

Use one of the online rent-vs-buy calculators. I like the one available from NerdWallet.com.

https://www.nerdwallet.com/mortgages/rent-vs-buy-calculator

This will give you an idea of the affordability of owning a home vs renting in the area in which you live or want to live.

Back to Jim from our example above.

His rental payment was $900 a month. His mortgage payment is $775 per month including his real estate taxes and insurance. One of his goals in buying his own home was to reduce his monthly housing expense and he succeeded. And don't forget about the advantages of homeownership that I noted above in Chapter one. Jim will now be building equity every month instead of a pile of rent receipts.

How do you know if you will be able to find a home within your budget?

Three steps to finding the right home within your budget.

- Step One - Have a good vision in mind about what features you need in a home.

- Step Two - Have an idea of a target price based on how much of a mortgage you can afford. Estimate the amount of cash you will need. This includes your down payment, closing costs, repairs, improvements, and moving expenses.

- Step Three - Compare your home needs with homes available in your price range to determine if you are on track.

Step One - Let's Start with Your Home Vision:

I'm making available "Your Home Vision Checklist" to help you with this step. It is available on my own secure website at the above link. Best to download and print it out to use for the following steps.

https://secureservercdn.net/45.40.152.13/rms.fa6.myftpupload.com/wp-content/uploads/2020/07/Your-Home-Vision-Checklist.pdf

Too many buyers go out looking at homes without a clear understanding of what they are looking for.

- You must keep in mind that you will sell at some point in the future. What features of the home that appeal to you may not appeal to future buyers? Be careful not to buy in the extreme to the point that you will have difficulty selling in the future.

- List specifics of what you need and what you think you want. Make a distinction between the two categories. List features that would be pluses and features that would be minuses.

- If more than one person is buying, each of you should do your own list and then compare and combine into one list.

Start with Basics:

- How big a home do you want? What square footage? Do you know what twelve hundred, fifteen hundred or two thousand square feet looks like? How big is your current home?

Remember that you have to pay heating and cooling costs and clean and maintain the home. The larger the home, the higher potential costs to heat, cool, clean, or maintain.

- How many bedrooms? Do you need one or more guest rooms? Bedrooms aren't for sleeping alone. You should take into consideration potential or alternative uses. Do you need a hobby room? I have one of our spare bedrooms as a model train room. Do you need a sewing or craft room. Do you need an office space?

Also, looking ahead when you sell the home, would one or two bedrooms be enough to appeal to enough buyers. Or, would a three-plus bedroom home attract more buyers in the future?

- How many bathrooms? How many people will live in the home, and can one bathroom meet your needs? Will there be times when more than one person has to use a bathroom. Thus, two full baths or one bath with another half bath may be more of a need than a want?

If you are buying a two story home, is it important to have the bathroom on the same floor as the bedrooms? Many older two story homes have the bath on the first floor and bedrooms on the second floor. That is very inconvenient. Does this matter to you? It might to buyers in the future when you go to sell.

Do you have a need for a tub? Some people like showers and can live without a tub. But what about whoever buys the home from you? Having a tub/shower combination appeals to more future buyers than a simple shower.

- How large a garage? How many bays in the garage for cars? How much stuff do you need to store in the garage? Many garages end up without room for a car due to storage needs.

Can you do with a one-car garage? Will it be enough for a vehicle plus storage of a lawn mower, garden tools, and bikes? Can you add a storage building somewhere to relieve the garage of storage? Thus a one-car garage may be enough?

- What style of home? Homes come in all sorts of styles. But, remember that what appeals to you may not appeal to buyers in the future when you go to sell. Contemporary homes look great in a magazine and even in person. But are they practical for everyday living? Will the style of the home limit potential buyers in the future?

- How many floors? Do you have any issues climbing stairs? Will you have guests staying with you who will require a guest room on the first floor? Perhaps a single story home would be most appropriate for you.

- What general location? Do you like an urban setting where you can walk to almost anything you want. You can skip the car and take urban transportation for shopping or entertainment?

Check out https://www.walkscore.com/. This is a website to see how an address rates on proximity to shopping and entertainment.

Do you like a more rural setting? We have beehives and a garden and, thus, like our rural setting. But, we are car dependent.

Remember that prices tend to be much higher the closer a home is to urban centers. If you work and play in an urban center you may need to check out suburban areas that have access to mass transit. That could help you find a home you can afford.

The more rural you go; the lower prices tend to be. Some mortgage loan programs are available only in rural areas. One such loan is from the US Department of Agriculture and requires no down payment.

- What age of home? Some older homes seem to have amazing charm. They don't make or design homes like they used to.

But, what is the condition of the older home? Is the electric updated? Is the plumbing updated? Is the heating system updated? How much work does the home need? Does it need cosmetic updates? Does it have structural or mechanical issues that will cost you a lot of money to update and/or to maintain?

- What school district? Check out: https://www.greatschools.org/ for information about schools in the area in which you want to live.

While school rankings are important it may be more important to visit schools. Go talk to administrators, teachers, and parents of children in the school. Get a feel for the learning atmosphere in the school district where you may buy a home.

You may already have your children in a school district and want to remain in that district.

If you don't have school age children you should still pay attention to this. Often times a home is more saleable and valuable in certain school districts over others. So checking out schools is important for any homebuyer to consider.

Consider Other Options:

- Swimming pool? Swimming pools are a mixed bag. Some people love them, and others hate them. Pools can be expensive to maintain. There is the potential for increased liability. You may have to install a safety fence or other preventive measures to restrict access.

What if you don't want a pool but you find the otherwise perfect home with an above-ground pool. Do you skip it or do what one of my clients did? She posted a notice at work that she would have an above-ground pool for sale for four hundred dollars. She pre-sold it in one day.

- Fenced yard? Do you have young children? Do you have a dog? You may want a fenced yard but could add one if needed including an Invisible Fence(TM) for dogs.

- Fireplace? Fireplaces need increased maintenance and mean safety concerns. You may have the idea that it would be nice to curl up in front of a fireplace on a cold winter night. But ask yourself about the condition of the chimney.

Does the chimney need a liner to prevent chimney fires? If the chimney has deteriorated or cracked hot embers could get into the structure of the home and cause a fire. When was the chimney last cleaned? Fireplace chimneys need cleaning and inspecting at least once per season.

Will a fireplace increase the cost of your insurance? Would a pellet stove be more practical. Would a wood burning-stove or pellet stove insert for the fireplace be better?

- Finished basement? Is the basement already finished? If you want to finish it, is the ceiling height enough to add a dropped ceiling? Is the basement dry enough to finish? If there are moisture issues, address them before adding improvements to the basement.

What about radon in the home? Nearby homes may not have radon issues, but your home may have elevated levels of radon.   Radon can be in the air and in the water if the home has a private well. If you are going to finish the basement, make sure to have it checked for radon. Include radon testing as part of the contingency process in your offer. If the test shows elevated radon levels you need to install a radon mitigation system.   Such a system is less expensive to install before finishing the basement.   It also could be a negotiation item so that the seller pays for the system.

Is there more than one means of ingress and egress from the basement? Many building and health codes mandate at least two methods of ingress and egress.   A finished off basement space must meet these codes if you want to use it as extra living space. Check on building codes to make sure that any finished basement meets codes. Or, that any planned improvements meet codes. Finished basements usually add to the value of a home.

- Air Conditioning? Does the home have good airflow to the extent that air conditioning isn't necessary? Does the home have a forced air heating system. This allows for the installation of air conditioning if it doesn't have one already.   If the home has a boiler or hot water heating system, air conditioning will have to be a separate system. Or, window air conditioning may do the job.

- Hardwood floors? Are they in good shape? Some people appreciate hardwood floors while others do not like them. How do you feel about them? Do you prefer carpet? Wood floors with throw rugs may work for you.

- Porch and/or Deck? We can appreciate sitting outside with a beverage in hand as we enjoy the evening sunset. Or enjoying a cookout with family and friends. Is a deck or porch a plus or a need in which to have a place to relax? Can you add a porch or deck?

Another idea is to list reasons why a feature is important to you.

For example, you may desire three bedrooms. Yet, you may intend to use one so-called bedroom as a den or office. A two-bedroom home with a separate den-office might meet your needs.

Go through the variables in this chapter and respond to each question. Ask yourself why you provided each response to dig deeper to learn how important each feature is to you.

Needs vs Wants:

It is important that you separate needs from wants. For example, you may want a two-car garage but only need a one-car garage. The two-car garage could be a real plus in your mind. But if the home with a one-car garage meets your other needs, it may end up being the available home you most desire. After all, you might be able to expand the garage into a two-car garage in the future.

Another example would be the desire or want to have a half bath on the first floor. There may be space on the first floor where a half-bath could live. For example, is there an extra closet or a bump-out into the garage where you could later install a half-bath? So even if a home doesn't have the half bath you prefer, you may decide that a home without it is your best choice.

Caution:

You should keep your options as open as possible. If you restrict your search to the ideal home, you may not have many options to choose from. You may become frustrated and stressed out with the process. Or, to get all the options you want the price may be out of your budget and beyond your affordable monthly payment.

Buyers should stay flexible to have enough homes to consider. Search on the least of features you consider absolute musts. Stay flexible on the rest. The ideal home might not exist, but many homes will come close if you remain flexible. Also, the ideal home may not be within your price range at the moment but could be in your price range as time passes.

You should be realistic about what you are about to buy. It is easy to get carried away with what you think you want. It is understandable. We see pictures of fancy homes in magazines and online. But, it is important for you to remain in touch with reality.

It is important to understand that the home you buy isn't the last home that you will ever own. It is better to buy within your means than to end up with buyer's remorse. Some of the homeowners in the Bankrate.com survey didn't follow that advice.

Step Two - Establish a price estimate to compare your home features to what is available.

You need to see if homes on the market are compatible with your needs.

This step involves coming up with a reasonable estimate of a price you can pay. Determine how much of a mortgage you can afford and add your down payment.

A cash flow analysis determines the amount of a mortgage you can qualify for.

This is generally figured by applying debt-to-income ratios.

As a rule of thumb, conventional financing requires a debt-to-income (DTI) ratio of 28/36. FHA and other forms of financing have their own requirements. They are often more liberal than 28/36. But using these numbers will provide a conservative estimate for use at this stage.

The first ratio is the ***"Front-End Ratio"***. A bank will allow up to 28% of your gross monthly income for your monthly mortgage payment. Note that this is your gross income before deductions for taxes, etc.

Your mortgage payment includes PITI.

Principal—the amount you pay back to the bank every month.

Interest—the profit you pay to the bank each month.

Taxes—the real estate property tax estimate for your home. Paid into an escrow account monthly so the bank can pay your real estate taxes when they are due.

Insurance—your fire and liability (homeowner) insurance plus PMI, Private Mortgage Insurance. You will pay PMI if your down payment is less than 20%.

The second ratio is the ***"Back-End Ratio"***. A bank will allow up to 36% of your gross monthly income for your mortgage payment PLUS other debt payments. These include your monthly payments for car loans, student loans, and credit cards. This does not include your rent as you would no longer have a rent payment after buying a home.

Your qualifying mortgage payment then is the lesser of the two ratios.

There are many mortgage calculators online today. One such calculator I recommend is from NerdWallet.
https://www.nerdwallet.com/mortgages/mortgage-calculator/calculate-mortgage-payment?trk=nw_gn1_4.0

This calculator uses figures you supply such as:

- City and state where you want to buy.

- Whether this is for you or for you and a spouse (partner).

- Your gross annual or monthly income.

- Your spouse's (partner's) gross annual or monthly income if applicable.

- Your monthly debt payments for car loans, student loans, and credit card payments.

- The amount of your anticipated down payment.

- An estimate of your FICO credit score range.

NerdWallet takes the information and comes up with a monthly payment figure.

It then determines an estimate for the price you would qualify for. Based on your income, the down payment you enter, and your debt to income ratios, you know where you stand..

My experience is homebuyers qualify for a higher mortgage than they want.

Take a serious look at what the calculator comes up with. Then stay on the conservative side and adjust the monthly payment lower. Work with a monthly figure YOU are comfortable with.

There is a button you move left to decrease the monthly payment or right to increase the monthly payment.

If your current monthly rent payment is $1,500. And the calculator comes up with a total payment, including taxes and insurance, of $2000 per month. That might be a stretch. So a more appropriate amount to use might be $1,400 to $1,700.

Also keep in mind that once you own a home you have other expenses that you don't have when you are renting.

Your decision should also take into consideration repairs and maintenance. You will have these owning a home vs renting a home where your rent generally includes such expenses.

With regard to utilities, if your rent includes utilities consider this as well. You are responsible for all utilities once you own your own home.

Consider this as you slide the button for the best monthly mortgage payment estimate to use. Caution: there are links all over the Nerdwallet.com website to get a mortgage quote from dozens of lenders. You aren't there yet so don't click on any of these.

Step Three - Goals (Needs) vs Reality:

Your next step is to see if your ideas line up with one another.

Do so by checking out homes for sale. You can check on the internet these days without calling a real estate licensee. You are not ready to interface with a real estate agent at this point.

https://www.realtor.com/ will give you the best up-to-date database of listed property anywhere in the country. Other options include trulia.com and zillow.com. These sites include homes that are for sale by owner, listed by an agent and not currently available for sale. This can be very confusing.

The other issue with trulia.com and zillow.com is lack of being up to date. I've had clients email or call me with listings they saw on trulia.com or zillow.com. Often they had sold and closed several months before or that weren't for sale at all.

Regardless of which online site you use, caution is in order:

WARNING:

Do not give out your email address, phone number, or other contact information. This will invite aggressive sales tactics by traditional real estate industry licensees-salespeople. It also provides a way for them to unscrupulously claim you are their buyer. Don't do it!

Online listing sites make their money by selling your information as leads for real estate salespeople. Local real estate company websites get your information for that company's salespeople.

Again, never provide your email or phone number at any of these online sites. Never click on the button that says "more information" or something similar. You are not ready to see these homes or any home at this point. You are still in the information gathering, preparation stage.

Be aware of a hidden industry concept called *"procuring cause"*.

This is a method by which a real estate salesperson can take advantage of the licensee you ultimately decide to work with. By signing in to any of the above websites or a local real estate brokerage site, the salesperson you make contact with can "*claim*" you as their buyer. This then allows the salesperson to later claim they are owed a commission even if you buy a home using another licensee. It is often used by unscrupulous salespeople to "*steal*" the commission that your ultimate licensee is paid. The next section, "*One Date You Are Married*", will explain this in more detail.

One Date You Are Married:

If you make contact with a real estate salesperson who supplies you with information about a property, they can make a claim to be paid a commission even though you purchase that property through another agent or even directly through the seller.

Welcome to a behind the scenes drama that plays out from time to time without buyers or sellers initially knowing what is happening.

- Have you signed-in and toured homes during open houses?

- Have you called real estate licensees for information about listings?

- Have you toured one or more homes with one or more salesperson or broker?

- Have you provided your e-mail address over the Internet to receive listing updates?

Then you may have unknowingly gotten married to an agent!

Unbelievable You Say?

Well, it's true.

If you make contact with a real estate salesperson or broker who supplies you with information about a property or who shows you a property, they can make a claim to be paid a commission even though you purchase that property through another agent or even directly through the seller.

That's right, even though you don't use that agent for a purchase of the property they showed you or gave you information about, they have a right to make a claim for a commission. You in essence have *"gotten married"* to that agent after one date or maybe just a handshake.

I guess love really is blind.

Of course you are free to use anyone you choose or no one at all to help you buy a home. But, if the home you buy was listed in a REALTOR® operated Multiple Listing System and if you were working with a real estate salesperson when you learned about that home or if a real estate salesperson gave you information about the home or showed you the home, that real estate salesperson can make a claim to be paid a commission.

They do this through REALTOR® arbitration but it could create a situation that results in you being sued for their commission plus legal costs.

How Can This Be, You Ask?

Blame it on the Realtor® Code of Ethics

Most real estate licensees are members of a REALTOR® Association and/or a REALTOR® run MLS (Multiple Listing Service). The term REALTOR® means a real estate licensee who is a member of NAR, the National Association of REALTORS®. As such they have to abide by the REALTOR® Code of Ethics.

This isn't a bad thing, really, in that you should want to do business with a real estate licensee who is professional and ethical and who agrees to practice according to a strict Code of Ethics.

However, this same Code of Ethics makes it mandatory for members to *"arbitrate business disputes"*.

The National Association of REALTORS® (NAR) Code of Ethics and Arbitration Manual, Article 17, states: *"In the event of contractual disputes or specific non-contractual disputes as defined in Standard of Practice 17-4 between REALTORS® (principals) associated with different firms, arising out of their relationship as REALTORS®, the REALTORS® shall submit the dispute to arbitration in accordance with the regulations of their Board or Boards rather than litigate the matter."*

When dealing with disputes having to do with real estate commissions, the method of determining who is entitled to the commission is a concept referred to as *"Procuring Cause"*. Or, in other words, who started the series of uninterrupted events that led to a successful transaction, i.e., a real estate transaction that closed?

You can see how a real estate salesperson who gives you information or shows you a home has a basis for a claim for commission. They feel that they alone *"started the series of uninterrupted events that led to a successful transaction"* and that they should be compensated for it regardless of whether or not they actually wrote the contract or did anything else to earn said commission.

OK, so what?

How does that involve me?

Isn't this a REALTOR® thing?

Well, not really, because…..

- You may not be able to find a buyer agent of your choice if you decide to be represented. A true buyer agent who is aware of the potential problems may not want to represent you because of the possibility that they may have their compensation taken away from them after the closing.

- You could be obligated to pay a buyer agent twice. If the previous licensee you contacted is awarded your buyer agent's compensation through REALTOR® Arbitration, your current agent may sue you for the compensation that was taken away from or never given to them.

- You could be sued by the seller. This primarily happens where buyers purchase a property that is listed with a "limited services broker". A limited services listing is one where the listing broker provides very limited services and many times only provides access to a local Realtor© multiple listing system at a discount but then provides no other services such as presenting or negotiating offers. With such a listing, the buyer negotiates directly with the seller rather than through the listing agent, unless they are represented by a buyer agent. If the buyer had contact with another agent previously, but who now is getting bypassed, that agent sometimes brings an arbitration action against the limited services broker to collect the compensation that was offered through the multiple listing system. If the listing broker loses, they will probably sue the seller to recover any money lost. These sellers then may turn around and sue you, the buyer, as you were the one who created the initial problem by not using the first agent to complete the sale.

What Should You Do?

- Decide if you are going to use the services of a professional buyer's agent rather than a real estate salesperson to help you purchase a home. Because if you are, you absolutely should start doing so as early in the process as possible to prevent problems for that agent in working for you.

- Be cautious about purchasing a home directly from the seller if it was for sale through a real estate salesperson at the time you learned about it or saw it. It is possible that you will get caught up in an arbitration situation and end up having to pay a real estate commission later plus legal costs. It is possible that the real estate salesperson you had contact with could also sue you directly claiming to be the procuring cause of your purchase of that home.

- Fully disclose the extent of any contact or relationship that you have had or have with any other real estate salespeople, if you have already had contact with one or more real estate licensees and now want to use the services of a new agent. It is important for the new agent to know whether or not he or she may have a problem with regard to a particular property that you may be interested in purchasing if you found out about it or obtained information about it or was shown it by another real estate licensee. There are steps that your new agent may be able to take that will reduce the risk of another real estate licensee making a claim that they are due a commission.

- Let the seller and their agent, if any, know about your contact with another agent if you decide to purchase a home working directly with a seller, who has or had the home listed with a limited services broker. This may help them avoid potential arbitration actions by the previous broker and lawsuits as noted previously.

Protect Your Interest!

You must take certain steps to protect your interest:

- If there is a home you actually are interested in purchasing, that you saw or found out about from a previous real estate salesperson, who you do not want to use now to buy that home, you must proceed with caution. This requires that you must protect your new agent's ability to keep their commission. Or, in the event you are buying directly from a seller, protect the seller's ability to work with you without being liable for a commission.

- You would need to inform the previous real estate salesperson (verbally and in writing) that you no longer wish to use their services. There is a provision in the NAR Code of Ethics Arbitration Procedures that refutes the first licensee's claim if it can be shown that there was either an "abandonment" or "estrangement" by them. Abandonment would mean that the real estate salesperson didn't follow up with you or that a lot of time goes by since they communicated with you. Estrangement would mean that the real estate salesperson, through their actions or words, made you decide not to use them.

- You should make one last contact with the previous licensee to end the "relationship" with them. I know, you may not have signed anything and thus feel that you have no obligation to the previous licensee and technically no actual relationship. It doesn't matter, that salesperson may think you are his buyer and that a relationship exists. End it nicely but firmly. Tell them in writing why you don't want to use their services. Make sure to give your new agent or the seller, if you are buying direct, a copy of the letter and make sure you don't have any further contact with the previous salesperson.

There are legitimate reasons why buyers do not or may not want to work with a particular real estate licensee after seeing one or more homes with them or getting information about various homes from them.

- Perhaps the real estate salesperson shows incompetence or inexperience.

- Perhaps they just don't seem attuned to your needs.

- Or maybe their personalities just plain clash with yours or they said or did something that you didn't like.

If that is the case, document such situations and keep a record of them for future reference just in case a problem does arise, end the relationship as noted above and go on.

However, where money is involved, sometimes greed takes over where common sense and fair play should be the norm.

If you are attempting to cut an agent out of a commission to supposedly save money by buying directly from a seller or by using another agent who will rebate some or all of their commission back to you, then expect problems.

If a real estate licensee has expended time and effort on your behalf and you have continued and encouraged the relationship, you do in fact owe a certain amount of allegiance to them. It is the moral and ethical thing to do.

To now attempt to take advantage of that licensee is just plain wrong and generally you will feel that in your gut. Such a decision is generally short sighted and probably will result in a lot of grief and lead to potential financial loss.

Think long and hard before taking such a route. If it is legitimate, document and end the relationship. If it is not, follow your moral instincts and do what is right. Either complete the deal with that licensee or tell them what you are planning and compensate the agent in some way.

Do's and Don'ts:

If you do plan on being in contact with several real estate agents:

- Do share confidential information about you and your ability to purchase a home *only with the licensee whom you choose to represent you as a buyer's agent.* If you share this information with other real estate licensees, they potentially could use this information against you if they represent the seller of a home that you want to buy.

- Don't get too involved with any real estate license until you are sure that is the person you wish to use to represent you in purchasing a home. The more deeply involved you get and the more homes you see with one real estate licensee, the easier it becomes for that licensee to claim to be the "procuring cause" on a future purchase by you of a property that you learned about or saw through that licensee, whether you purchase that home through another agent or directly from the seller.

- Don't sign any written documents, except mandatory agency disclosures, with any real estate licensee except the one you choose to be your buyer agent.

- Do make it very clear from the beginning that you are interviewing several agents before deciding to use the services of one exclusively. Sellers generally interview two or three or more listing agents asking for proposals and marketing plans before they choose which agent to use. You can do the same, as long as you do so cautiously.

- Don't leave your e-mail address, phone number, or mailing address with any real estate company or licensee. To do so invites more aggressive and potentially irritating marketing efforts by such companies or licensees and potentially begins the process of a real estate licensee being able to claim "procuring cause". If you are asked to "sign-in" at an open house, give your name, but don't leave your address or phone number. Take the licensee's business card and say that if you are interested further you will contact them.

- Don't continue or encourage the development of a relationship with a real estate salesperson who you probably don't want to actually buy your home from in the future. It is unfair to them and may lead to problems later for you or your new agent. If you are contacted by a real estate licensee that you are pretty sure you don't want to use as your buyer agent, politely but firmly ask them to stop contacting you. Ask them to remove your phone number or e-mail address from their records. The more you encourage the development of a relationship with one real estate licensee, the more difficult it becomes for you in the future if you decide to hire another licensee as your buyer agent.

OK, Do homes in your price range appear to have features and options that you want and that you can afford?

The goal of this chapter was to answer the question, "

Will you be able to find a home you like within your budget?"

If it appears that your needs match reality, congratulations. You may be ready to continue and can skip the next chapter. But, if they don't or you feel that you would like to stretch a bit further, you need to take some more steps. The next chapter will cover this in more detail.

Chapter Five
Should You Wait to be
in a Better Buying Position?

We discussed cash needs in Chapter Two.

- Are you satisfied that you have enough cash saved up currently?

- Do you need some more time in which to maximize your savings?

- Do you need to add to your emergency funds before proceeding with buying a home?

- You may have to or want to wait several months or more to build up more money. This could be for a larger down payment. Or, to pay off some debts so you can afford a larger monthly payment.

We discussed credit and credit issues in Chapter Three.

- Are you comfortable that your FICO credit scores are at their highest?

- Have you improved them as much as you reasonably can?

- You may need more time to improve your credit scores. This may allow you to get lower interest rate. That would allow you to buy a more expensive home that might meet your needs better.

- Lenders determine an interest rate based on a combination of a FICO score and cash down payment. Waiting a few months so that you can increase both your down payment and FICO scores, might be well worth the wait.

We discussed your vision and needs vs wants in Chapter Four.

You may need to adjust your features list and consider a less ideal home.

Take a look at the homes that are coming up in the price range you decided on based on your monthly budget.

- Do they need too much work?

- Are they way off from what you can live with?

- What adjustments can you make to your needs list that might allow you to consider homes in this price range?

You may have to find a way to get up into a higher price range to meet your vision and needs.

- Check online again to see what the price range is of homes that better meet your needs.

- Is this within your range of possibilities? It may not be currently.

- But with some serious planning and focus, it could be. You may want to delay buying a home for six months or a year.

Don't throw caution to the wind and buy a home that you can't afford or that may not meet your basic needs or wants.

- Remember your peers with buyer's remorse.

- Make sure your needs are in line with your financial abilities.

- Be realistic, and you will feel much better about your homebuying adventure.

Here are some more considerations:

How stable is your employment and source of income?

There currently is a lot of uncertainty in the economy during the Covid-19 pandemic. People collecting unemployment insurance is at the highest it has been in a very long time.

How stable is your job? Are you in a job that is deemed "essential"? Are you able to work from home? What are the long-term prospects for the business you are in?

There is a lot of uncertainty going on right now. We have experienced failed leadership on both the federal and on many state levels. We have an important election coming up soon. No one really knows where things are heading. Perhaps "caution" is the word of the day. My advice is to wait this stuff out.

If two or more of you will make the decision, get on the same page, and stay there.

I've had couples look at certain homes, and right away, I knew they did not think along the same lines. I had to review their needs and wants list with them to find common ground between them. The review saved much time and effort as they looked at homes.

Sometimes one person will dominate search criteria and the choice of homes we look at.

You may regret buying a home that one party likes, and the other doesn't.

I had a couple that wanted to buy a fixer-upper. After the transaction closed, I learned that he wanted the fixer-upper. She wanted a ready-to-move-into-home. She never expressed that during our time together. She blamed me for pushing them into a fixer-upper. He dominated the process, and she suffered.

It is best to find common ground and compromises, or you shouldn't buy a home and instead, continue renting. At least with renting, your commitment amounts to one year or less.

- Buying a home usually comes with a commitment to a thirty-year mortgage.

- Without taking a big financial hit, it usually isn't easy to sell a home within a year or two.

- You may end up living in a home that doesn't meet your needs.

- If you are a dating couple you may think it would be great to own a home together.

Make sure you are ready for the financial commitment of borrowing money together to buy a home. I've had clients who decided to split up as we processed a contract to buy a home. They tried to use the home inspection contingency to get out of the contract. But the home had nothing wrong to warrant their doing that. They refused to go through with buying the home and lost their contract deposit.

Rather than face such a loss, rent for a while, and make sure that living together and paying joint bills works. Do this before you buy a home and take on a thirty-year mortgage commitment together. It might be better to have a month-to- month or one-year lease obligation than a thirty-year mortgage.

Rent-To-Own

People often rent-to-own a TV, a computer or other household goods. It can work also for buying a home. A rent-to-own, also known as a lease/option, agreement allows you to lease a home that you have the "option" to purchase later when you are able.

I believe that a lease/option can be a good way to go in certain circumstances. First, is the home one that you would be interested in buying if you were able to get a mortgage and close currently? Second, are you sure that whatever is holding you back from qualifying for a mortgage and closing currently can be overcome within the lease term.

As a real estate investor I often purchase homes with the express purpose of doing a lease/option to someone who is experiencing some of the issues discussed above. The tenant/buyer and I must be relatively sure they are going to do what it takes to get into a position to qualify for a mortgage and close within the lease term.

My lease/options usually involve a two to three year lease term giving the tenant/buyer enough time to be able to close. My lease/option program looks for tenant/buyers for whom a cash down payment isn't an issue. I generally seek a non-refundable down payment upfront of $10,000 or more. The tenant/buyer is required to handle all repairs, maintenance and improvements. The tenant also is required to pay all utilities including water, sewer and trash.

The advantage for a tenant/buyer is that they are living in a home that ultimately in the near future will be theirs. In the meantime, any improvements they make will benefit them in the long term and not a landlord. They also lock-in a future purchase price that is good during the lease/option term. It also gives them the incentive to do what it takes to tackle the issues that are holding them back from purchasing currently.

For more information go to my rent-to-own website for an idea of how it works.

https://rent-to-own-your-own-home.com/

Chapter Six
Do you Know Who
to Trust and Work With?

Be forewarned.

*This chapter is long. It contains information that you won't find anywhere else. Want the best outcome for your homebuying adventure? You need to pay attention to this material in particular. It can make a world of difference. Will you become one of the homeowners who regrets buying their home? Or, will you become a homeowner who is confident they made the right choices? Remember, I'm an exclusive buyer agent providing true fiduciary duties to homebuyers only. This book is written from that mindset. I'm not a salesperson and won't tell you something that I think you **want to hear**. I only tell people what they **need to hear**.*

The traditional real estate industry has an ingrained sales culture. As a result who can you trust?

When a real estate licensee claims to be a buyer agent, will the licensee actually be your agent? Or, are they telling you something you want to hear, but that they are unwilling or unable to provide? They have a salesperson's mindset.

How does one find an "agent"?

The general answer is to find a real estate licensee who:

- Is familiar with the local area.

- Has several years of experience.

- Has some industry specific designations such as GRI, CRS, ABR, CBR.

- Who you heard about from friends, relatives, or work associates.

There is a problem with these approaches. Everyone knows someone who is "in the real estate business". I bet you know at least one person licensed and in real estate. So do your friends, relatives, or work associates.

I bet they didn't have the advantage that you will have. You have the opportunity to understand what you should be considering before working with any agent. Because that is what I will be covering in this chapter.

How do you know that the real estate licensee they recommend or the one that you know is in fact a true agent?

Do you even know what a true agent is?

- Sure, they may have a license. Sure, they call and advertise themselves as a real estate "agent". Sure, you or your relatives, friends and work associates refer to them as agents. But that doesn't mean that they actually can or will represent you as a true legal fiduciary agent.

- Real estate licensees refer to themselves as agents. In most instances they aren't your agent but rather an agent for the seller. Or, not an agent at all but rather a salesperson. To reduce confusion, I like to refer to them as salespersons or licensees rather than agents.

- You have to dig deeper and find out if they will represent your best interests at all times and in every situation. Do this before you have one of them help you buy a home.

- A home is the largest expense you will have in your lifetime. Deciding who to work with needs considerable thought.

- Experience, familiarity with the area and industry specific training and certifications are important. But, these aren't the most important criteria to use.

- You need someone to represent, protect and advocate for you. *Is that in fact what you want*? I assume it is.

- You need someone willing and able to take on the legal role and liability as your true agent.

- You don't want a salesperson or someone with a salesperson's mindset.

7 out of 10 homebuyers use the first agent they come in contact with.

Often that agent is the listing agent. And, 85% of homebuyers start their search for a home online. They spend hours researching what homes are available. Yet they spend little time thinking about, researching, or interviewing real estate licensees. That is a huge and costly mistake.

The most important issue when buying a home is knowing what makes an agent, an agent.

Find someone who will guarantee to be your agent and not an agent when it is convenient to be one. Avoid the real estate licensee who uses the term as a sales tactic. They have no idea what the terminology, "buyer agent" or "fiduciary", means.

Homebuyers I work for want to buy the right home at the right price.

They don't want to have someone SELL them a home. Look at traditional real estate industry ads. You see agents bragging about their million-dollar sales production. They push their latest hot listing for sale. And, you see lots of SOLD signs.

The same salespeople turn around and tell you how one of them can be your buyer's agent and save you lots of money. We should not believe them!

I remember a display ad many years ago by a traditional real estate salesperson. It contained photos of a dozen of her listings around the outside of the ad. On the inside of the ad she had a statement. It was about the tens of thousands of dollars she had saved buyers as their buyer's agent.

That ad didn't last long. Imagine being a seller considering listing a home with her. Would they want to use a real estate licensee who brags about saving buyers thousands of dollars?

Why would buyers want to use a salesperson who brags about their million-dollar sales? It doesn't make sense either.

Most real estate licensees work in an office where agents take listings and work with buyers.

They have ongoing relationships with one another. We can't trust that their loyalty to you and your home buying is greater than their loyalty to their office. Or, to their coworkers when dealing with an in-house deal!

You want the lowest price and best terms, and the seller wants the highest price and best terms. The real estate company wants to make a deal and double-end a commission. They get this from both the sell side and buy side of the transaction. They often pay a higher commission split to its agents for an in-house sale.

To help complete an in-house deal, real estate salespeople share information.

They share their buyers' and sellers' needs and qualifications. They do so in passing or at sales meetings or over lunch or coffee.

Is it to your advantage to have your so-called agent sharing how much you can pay? Or, how much cash you have for a down payment? Or, that your lease is up in two months and you have to move and need to buy yesterday?

This is confidential information. It reduces your ability to negotiate for a better deal, if shared with the other side.

Do you believe there is no chance you will be short-changed on an in-house deal?

What does it mean for a real estate licensee to be your agent?

Words have meanings.

An agency is a legal relationship. One person, "an agent", works for another, "a principal", a/k/a "a client". The agent agrees to act on the principal/client's behalf and in their best interest.

Relationships you have with an attorney are like this.

Attorneys, by law, must be loyal to you and look out for your best interest at all times. They are your "fiduciary" and your agent, and you are their "client". They owe you the full range of fiduciary duties. They avoid conflicts of interest. If they identify a conflict they withdraw from representing you.

Several years ago, I referred a buyer client to a real estate attorney. I had to find a different attorney with a different law firm. A conflict appeared with regard to someone else in his law firm, who was no longer with the firm. He had ten years before represented the child of the seller whom my buyer client was buying a home from. That created a conflict of interest and thus the attorney had to recuse himself.

Law firms do this all the time. They have a robust "conflict of interest" policy and process to avoid such situations. That is true agency, true fiduciary representation. It makes sense. Say you were suing someone. Would you want the same or another attorney in the law firm you are using representing the person you are suing? Of course not!

It is unethical for a law firm to represent two clients against one another.

Unfortunately, that isn't true with the real estate industry.

Hard to imagine a traditional real estate industry brokerage taking that same approach. They should refer a buyer out to another brokerage when an in-house deal arises. Then the buyer can get true representation without conflicts of interest. Of course they don't. The profit potential of doing in-house deals is too great.

Wise words from a former General Counsel to the NYS Department of State:

"Stop calling yourselves 'agents' unless you are an agent within the meaning of centuries of well-settled common law."

So stated Maureen Glasheen, Esq., a former General Counsel to the NY State Department of State. This was in a recent email to myself and others in a consumer advocacy online group. She continued:

"ONLY persons and firms who transact business as follows meet the definition of Agent. Their actions are subject to our lawful instruction. They operate SOLELY IN OUR BEST INTEREST, (a/k/a Undivided Loyalty) at all times."

"Terms like Dual Agent and Designated Agent describe variations on DISLOYALTY. These are not a service option."

"Agents misuse the term 'Agent' to mis-describe their role. They do this to induce the trust and confidence of prospective clients. If done without intent to offer Undivided Loyalty they may be engaging in consumer fraud."

A real estate licensee can function as a true fiduciary like an attorney, which is very rare. Or they function as a salesperson playing, "let's make a deal".

I know the primary reason why homeowners surveyed by Bankrate.com ended up with buyer's remorse.

They regretted buying their home by ignoring the concept of agency. They did not use true fiduciary representation. They failed to use a real estate licensee who was their legal agent. In essence, someone SOLD them a home. They bought their home the same way they buy a car, through a salesperson.

A salesperson doesn't care if the buyer is paying too much. They don't care if you buy the wrong home, or buy a home you can't afford, or later regret buying a home. Their focus is on making a sale and getting a commission. If they can double-end a deal and sell a listing to an in-house buyer, all the better!

Most real estate licensees are good people with good intentions.

I'm not saying that individual licensees are evil. They don't mean to short-change buyers. Yet, state law requires real estate licensees place their licenses with a brokerage. The brokerage is the entity that determines the business model. The individual licensees must then adhere to what the brokerage tells them to do. So, an individual licensee may want to be a true agent, but due to the brokerage's business model, they can't be. It is the deeply ingrained sales culture of the entire real estate industry that is the problem.

Do you know what the term "fiduciary" means and what "fiduciary duties" an agent should owe to you?

Most real estate licensees don't know, but you should.

There is a body of law that goes back 200 years called "common law". It originated in England and brought over to the US 200+ years ago as the foundation for our own laws. It has changed over the years. Legislative changes and lawsuit decisions by state and federal courts modified the law. It provides us with the framework within which we all operate.

Part of the common law has to do with agency and trusts from which real estate representation stems. The most important aspect of this is that *"one can't serve two masters"*. This is a principle that the traditional real estate industry has ignored. They outright abandoned the concept.

A trustee (referred to as the agent/fiduciary) owes "Undivided Loyalty". They also owe other fiduciary duties, to their principal (referred to as the client).

The highest legal duty of one party to another is being a fiduciary.

This requires being bound to act in the other's best interests in an ethical manner.

If you want the best outcome to your homebuying adventure you better pay attention.

- You need to understand what a true agent is.

- You must demand that the real estate licensee you use adhere to the common law.

- They must provide full fiduciary duties to you.

- They must guarantee and pledge their loyalty to you, without exception.

The acronym OLDCAR describes the fiduciary duties owed to you by a true agent.

- Obedience to Lawful Instruction.

Requires the agent to act subject to your continuous control. The agent must follow your lawful instructions.

- Undivided Loyalty.

Prohibits the agent from advancing any interests that are adverse to your own. This is impossible when one or more real estate licensees try to work both sides of a deal. They cannot provide undivided loyalty as they have compromised it to both parties. They are attempting to help a buyer get the lowest price and best terms for themselves. They are attempting to help a seller get the highest price and best terms for themselves. And, in the process they make a deal that provides a double commission for themselves. The buyer and seller have opposing goals and adverse interests. The agents can't be loyal to either party.

- Full Disclosure of Material Information.

Requires the agent to disclose all information which might impact your best interest. This includes the seller's motivation for selling and the price the seller paid for the home. It includes disclosing potential deferred maintenance or defects in the home. Your agent should provide price comparisons for similar homes. They should give you the listing and sale history of the home.

- Confidentiality.

Prohibits the agent from disclosing confidential information obtained from you. This includes the price you are willing to pay and the amount of mortgage you qualify for. It includes how much cash you have to work with or the level of your motivation to buy a particular home.

- Accountability.

Requires the agent to account for all money received, e.g. escrow deposits.

- Reasonable Skill and Care.

Requires the agent to protect you from foreseeable risks. The agent should refer you to get expert advice when your needs are outside the scope of the agent's expertise.

Financial Services Industry and Fiduciary Representation.

Have you seen the TV ads by Fisher Investments? A woman or a man is sitting at their desk. They say,

"At Fisher Investments we do things differently and other money managers don't understand why."

We then see a man walking toward the camera and saying,

"Because our way works great for us."

Then back to the woman or man at the desk who says,

"But not for your clients. That's why we're fiduciaries, obligated to put clients first."

Fisher Investments is an RIA, Registered Investment Adviser.

"For over 40 years, Fisher Investments has worked in our clients' best interests. We think and act independently rather than follow outdated industry practices."

From their website, https://www.fisherinvestments.com/en-us:

"Fiduciary Defined. At its most basic level, a fiduciary is a person or firm who acts for clients and puts their best interests first at all times. RIAs register with the Securities and Exchange Commission (SEC) or the states in which they do business. In either case, they are held to the fiduciary standard to act in clients' best interests. We put clients first. We do

things differently than other investment firms. Not to be different, but because it makes a difference for our clients. We designed our entire business to minimize conflicts of interest."

Fisher Investments is a rare find in the financial services industry. As are True Loyal Agents(R), described later in this chapter, in the traditional real estate industry. You have a choice of working with a salesperson or a fiduciary. Between a stock broker or a registered investment adviser. Between a real estate salesperson or a true agent/fiduciary - True Loyal Agent(R).

The traditional real estate industry caused the abandonment of true representation years ago. The real estate industry was never as greedy and deceiving as it is today.

Back in 1986. From the NAR, the National Association of REALTORS(R), Publication, "Who Is My Client? A REALTORS(R) Guide to Compliance with the Law of Agency".

"The legal concept of Agency is most fundamental as applied to the real estate profession. It is the very nature and function of the real estate broker, appraiser, and manager to be an agent. The law of agency defines us and gives real estate practitioners their identity."

Even in 1993. From the NAR Publication, "Agency Choices, Challenges & Opportunities – Agent's Guide".

"Agency relationships make up the foundation of the real estate industry. One reason NAR formed was to enhance the professionalism of real estate brokers. They recognized an agency relationship between the broker and her client. They started educating all parties about the duties imposed by the relationship."

So the real estate industry did embrace the concept of true agency and fiduciary duties, once upon a time.

SO WHAT HAPPENED?

Why does the term "Agent" no longer mean "fiduciary" or "true legal agency"?

We should blame the ingrained sales culture of the traditional real estate industry.

"How to Defeat Mega Agents" and "Broken Industry" author Ryan Fletcher has a term he uses to describe agents. In his eyes they are "low-information agents".

"The 'Guru Party' and what they teach are bankrupting the real estate industry of trust. The Guru party, made up of; the trainers, brokers & endless supply of coaches are to blame. Because of them, the term 'real estate agent' in the eyes of society has become a stain on your reputation."

Here's a timeline that might shed some light on what happened:

From the beginning until the mid-1980's. Real estate licensees represented the seller. The seller was a "client" and the buyer was a "customer". Real estate licensees who worked with buyers were "seller sub-agents", representing the seller. They did not represent the buyer. There is a big difference between being a "customer", think car buying, vs. a "client", think attorney.

Then came the 1983 FTC, Federal Trade Commission's survey of real estate consumers. The survey revealed and exposed that home buyers were being misled. They believed they had a true agent, when by law they didn't. The agent showing them homes was the legal sub-agent of the sellers. The agent's actions led buyers (and sellers) to believe the agents represented the buyer.

Then came individual state agency disclosures. These explained the relationships between licensees and consumers. Real estate licensees had to decide and disclose their proposed relationship with consumers. Real estate licensees started to become familiar with the concept of agency.

Next came the educated homebuyer wanting to work with a buyer agent. They started asking for real estate licensees to be their agent. Homebuying books touted the advantage of buyers using their own agent. Even HUD, the US Housing and Urban Development agency, recommended using such a true agent.

Then came the need for traditional sales agents to market themselves as buyer agents. This was to meet the demand of buyers. They had to find a way to satisfy the buyer's needs.

But, then came the dilemma for traditional real estate salespeople. How do they deal with the in-house transaction and the fiduciary concept of, "One Can't Serve Two Masters"? Oops...The industry had embraced the concept of true representation. But they now had huge conflicts of interest doing an in-house deal.

They had to disclose to a buyer and a seller they no longer could provide true representation to either. They had to take a neutral position and more or less handle the paperwork instead of being a true agent. This did not go over well with smart buyers who wanted true representation.

Then came the watering down, and in some cases – elimination, of true agency. This became the solution rather than the transparency of disclosing conflicts of interest.

The National Association of Realtors is the second largest lobbyist group in the US. They wield much power when it comes to legislation and politics. They also influence the state commissions and departments of real estate. These agencies oversee the industry.

Many states now allow practices that hide conflicts of interest and deceive consumers. These legislative changes allow for the in-house double-dip of commissions. This is under the guise that consumers are still represented. And, that conflicts of interest no longer exist.

One outlandish example of consumer deception is in Florida.

The presumption in Florida is that all real estate licensees are "transaction brokers". They owe no fiduciary duties to consumers. Officials claim 95% of real estate licensees in Florida operate as transaction brokers.

Here is what the Florida Transaction Broker Notice says in part.

"Parties are giving up their rights to the undivided loyalty of the licensee. A licensee facilitates a real estate transaction. They assist both the buyer and the seller. A licensee will not work to represent one party to the detriment of the other party"

Do you think buyers and sellers are aware that their so-called agent in Florida isn't an agent at all. On July 1, 2008, the disclosure rule went away. So buyers and sellers think they have an agent when in most cases, they don't.

Transaction brokerage started in Florida, and now expanded to many other states. It is a way to avoid legal liability for a real estate licensee's actions. It protects the brokerage they are with.

If a buyer or seller gets harmed, the basis for a legal action is a "breach of fiduciary duty".

If a licensee "by law" isn't an agent they aren't providing fiduciary duties. Thus, they aren't held liable for a breach of such duties.

A local Florida real estate attorney writes in his blog.

"A lot of bad acts have happened in the Florida real estate market in recent years. Having an agent with the legal duty to act as a fiduciary can make all the difference. It is a matter whether someone wronged gets compensated for their damage. It is a limitation on the liability of a real estate agent and their broker to be able to act as a transaction broker. Instead of the full liability provided by an actual agent – a fiduciary. How important that duty may be to you will not become clear unless and until you experience harm. Buyers and sellers don't understand how important having an agent as a fiduciary is. That is until a catastrophe happens. And, they are meeting with a Florida real estate lawyer to try and find justice."

The attorney's words aren't applicable to Florida alone.

"Having an agent with the legal duty to act as a fiduciary can make all the difference. It is a matter whether someone wronged gets compensated for their damage."

You should heed this attorney's advice and make sure you are in-fact working with a true agent.

The real estate industry won't change unless you, the homebuyer, demands that it changes.

Don't ignore the concept of agency and true fiduciary representation. Don't look at houses with a real estate salesperson without regard to this concept. If you do, then the real estate industry will continue to take advantage of homebuyers. You deserve better.

A Different Mindset and Skillset!

Representing a buyer takes a different mindset and skillset than marketing and selling a home for a seller.

Legendary Real Estate Trainer Says Take A Stand, & Pick A Side

Mike Ferry released a report in August of 2014 suggesting agents pick one side of the transaction.

"I believe the skill set of an agent who works with buyers is completely different than the skill set of an agent who works on listings. Yes, they both have fundamental skills that all salespeople need ... the ability to manage your time, the ability to follow up on leads, the ability to prequalify, the ability to present, etc."

Ferry went on to state:

"... The skill set of a listing agent and buyer's agent are different from that point forward, meaning the ability to present in a fashion that causes a buyer or seller to sign a contract. ... I (have thought) for years that when an agent gets their license they should have to actually declare, 'I want to work with buyers' or 'I want to work with sellers.' The majority of agents do not have the total package of skill sets to do both and, in most cases, aren't willing to learn them because they are so vast and ... if they chose one and learned it well and practiced

it … they could, then, possibly in the future learn the other one.''

From Bernice Ross, CEO of RealEstateCoach.com, a national speaker, author and trainer with over 1,000 published articles and two best-selling real estate books.

"Sadly, the majority of agents lack the skills to do either job well.

The truth is that you need to work with a true agent who not only is loyal to you but who also has the right mindset and skillset to help you achieve your goals.

The True Loyal Agent(R)

The costliest mistake homebuyers make is using the wrong agent. Using the right agent, someone who is an agent not in name only, could save you thousands of dollars. This will provide you with the best outcome to your home buying adventure.

The right agent for you to use is one who is a True Loyal Agent(R). Someone who has the legal obligation to be your protector. To be loyal to you alone and look out for your best interest at all times and in every situation.

You don't want to use someone who uses the term "buyer agent" as a sales tactic. This is to deceive you into believing you are being represented when you aren't.

I've trademarked and registered the name True Loyal Agent(R). It refers to a real estate licensee/true agent. They are with a company that represents real estate consumers as true agents. Their business model removes conflicts of interest for their clients just as Fisher Investments does for their clients.

A True Loyal Agent(R) is always loyal, always a true agent.

Do you know a US Marine? Parhaps you are a US Marine yourself (*Thank you for your service*). The US Marine Corps motto is "Semper Fidelis". Ask a Marine what it means. You will hear,

"Always Faithful, Always Loyal." Ask them if there are any exceptions and you will hear, "NO. NEVER."

This is the kind of attitude that a True Loyal Agent(R) has when helping clients buy their homes.

- A True Loyal Agent(R) is a real estate licensee with a real estate firm which embraces, accepts, and adheres to the common law of agency.

- A True Loyal Agent(R), similar to a representative at Fisher Investments, does things differently than other traditional real estate licensees/salespeople. Not just to be different, but because it makes a difference for their clients. Their entire business is designed to minimize conflicts of interest.

- A True Loyal Agent(R) is always your true fiduciary, your protector, and loyal to you alone.

- A True Loyal Agent(R) will always be faithful to you and look out for your best interest at all times and in every situation. With no exceptions and no excuses.

- A True Loyal Agent(R) guarantees their undivided loyalty to you. They do this by not getting involved with in-house deals. Such licensees reject the ingrained sales culture of the traditional real estate industry. They reject the double-dipping of commissions. They reject the industry's insider wheeling and dealing, and bait and switch tactics.

Insider Self Dealing!

I recently represented a couple buying a home in central Massachusetts. They had seen a home during an open house some six months before meeting with me. They weren't quite ready to buy a home at that time. Now that they were ready to buy and their first thought was about the home they saw before.

I checked and found that it was still available. A previous deal had died due to the buyer not being able to get a mortgage. I went to set up a showing along with a couple of other homes.

But discovered that in the meantime its status had changed from active to contingent.

The sale was subject to the buyer getting a mortgage, home inspections and the sale of the buyer's home.

In such circumstances it is customary to have a "bump-out" clause. If another acceptable offer comes along that is not subject to the sale of a home, the seller has an option. The seller can serve notice on the first buyer to remove their home sale contingency. If the first buyer doesn't, their contract gets cancelled and the second buyer's offer is now valid.

I inquired about the bump provision and discovered there was none. My immediate suspicion was that this was an in-house deal. The listing agent, let's call her Suzy Salesperson, also was the one with the buyer.

Turns out it was worse than that. Suzy Salesperson was the listing agent on this property but also on another property. The buyer she had was the seller of the other property.

Suzy Salesperson was attempting the tri-fecta, a triple-dip of commissions. The listing commission on the one deal and both the buy and sell sides on the other deal. Whose interest do you think she was looking out for?

Anyway, shortly thereafter this second deal died as well, to our delight of course. It seems that the buyer had to cancel because their buyer walked away from the sale of their home. Thus they couldn't get a mortgage to complete the transfer.

Of course Suzy Salesperson lost out on her attempt to triple-dip commissions. But, that didn't stop her from continuing to attempt an in-house deal even when my client had it under contract. Her negotiating style showed she wasn't looking out for her seller client. Suzy Salesperson was hoping our deal would die so she could do another in-house deal.

Yes, my couple managed to buy the home at a good price and are very happy living there today. But this example shows you what can happen when there is an in-house transaction. It opens up the potential for self-dealing, conflicts of interest, and unethical behavior.

Some True Loyal Agents(R) represent homebuyers only as "Exclusive Buyer's Agents".

"True exclusive buyer's agents never take listings and never represent sellers. They don't work for a company that does. They never operate as dual agents, designated agents, transaction brokers, or facilitators. These are deceptive and disloyal relationships. They never get involved in an in-house transaction. They provide the full range of fiduciary duties at all times and in every situation to buyers only."

Some True Loyal Agents(R) represent buyers and sellers. But never in the same transaction. They are known as "Single-Party Agents".

"Single-party agents work for buyers and sellers, but never in the same transaction. Single-party agents never operate as dual agents, designated agents, transaction brokers, or facilitators. These are deceptive and disloyal relationships. Single-party agents and their offices follow strict procedures. They make sure that their buyer and seller clients are never represented at the same time."

Single-party agents make sure none of their current listings interest a buyer. If one or more of their listed properties interest you, they will not be able to take you on as a client. They will refer you to someone outside of their firm to represent you if that is what you would like. Or you could continue to buy their listing as a customer, not a client and without representation. If you have no interest in any of the firm's current listings they can take you on as a client as your True Loyal Agent(R).

As a buyer client of a single-party agency, if a seller wants to list a home, they will check to see if it is a home you might want. If so, they won't take on the seller as a client. They will encourage the seller to find someone else to list with. Or, to sell as a "for sale by owner," working with an attorney for help. If you want to buy the home, they will continue representing you as a client as your True Loyal Agent*(R)*.

A single-party agent operates as a True Loyal Agent*(R)* at all times and in every situation. They operate like a law firm. A law firm represents sellers and buyers of real estate but never in the same transaction. If a law firm had a previous relationship with a seller, the law firm would not be able to also represent a buyer. I gave an example of that before.

How do you know if you are talking to a True Loyal Agent*(R)*?

Ask if the licensee-salesperson or anyone else in their company takes listings. If they do, they aren't an exclusive buyer's agent or with an exclusive buyer agency.

But, the licensee-salesperson may still be a True Loyal Agent*(R)*. You have to ask the next question to see if the licensee is a true single-party agent.

Will you still try to represent me if I want to buy a home listed by you or someone else in your company?

If they claim it is possible to represent both the seller and you they are not a true single-party agent. If you continue working with such a salesperson you could end being short-changed. You don't want to do that.

Why Should You Care?

A True Loyal Agent*(R)* has chosen to provide a higher level of duties, service, and ethics. A traditional real estate licensee can't match that. A True Loyal Agent*(R)* embraces their fiduciary role and willingly takes on the legal liability that being a fiduciary agent entails. The traditional real estate firm and their agents do everything to avoid legal liability, even if it results in deception or consumer fraud. They know that it is unlikely that a consumer will attempt to sue them.

You will never find a True Loyal Agent(R) operating in a traditional real estate brokerage.

- These offices encourage in-house transactions.

- They encourage working with buyers AND sellers in the same transaction.

- They practice dual or designated agency, transaction brokerage or act as a facilitator. These are the most common forms of In-House Dealing. I describe these below.

- These are all examples of disloyalty. They give you a false sense of trust and an illusion that you have an agent protecting you, when you don't.

Can a True Loyal Agent(R) guarantee you can save money by using them?

No. Let's face it, no one can guarantee actual savings. Every deal is different. Some people try to demonstrate savings by comparing the sale price to the list price. But there are so many variables with this approach it is useless.

Take a home that is worth $195,000. The list price is $210,000. You buy it for $205,000. You saved $5,000, right? No, you overpaid by $10,000 (Sale price of $205,000 minus the home's value of $195,000 equals $10,000 overpayment).

Say the list price is $180,000. You buy it for $190,000. You overpaid by $10,000, right? No, you underpaid by $5,000 (Home's value of $195,000 less the sale price of $190,000 equals $5,000 underpayment).

Where did I come up with the home's value being $195,000? Is the value of the home exactly equal to $195,000? No, a home is worth what a willing seller and willing buyer, with neither under pressure, agree it is worth. So trying to compare sale price and list price doesn't give us a true comparison of an agent's worth.

A True Loyal Agent(R) <u>CAN</u> guarantee their loyalty.

There is value knowing that the real estate licensee you are using is a true fiduciary. That they by law commit to looking out for your best interest. Without exception and without excuses.

I posed the question, "Who can you trust?". If you are putting that trust in someone who has a salesperson mindset, are you sure you want to do that? First-time homebuyers shouldn't. If you have purchased and sold a couple of homes you have the experience to take care of yourself. But if you "don't know what you don't know" and put your trust in a salesperson, good luck.

Instead, put that trust in someone who has a fiduciary mindset. Look for someone whose very business model eliminates conflicts of interest. There is value in this. It is in essence, "priceless". So when contemplating who to use to help you buy your home, keep this in mind. The value is in knowing the person you are using has your back.

In-House Dealing

The in-house transaction is the breeding ground for unethical behavior.

These real estate licensees are salespeople looking to sell you a home.

Ask yourself.

"Are you dealing with someone who is a fiduciary and who you can trust? Or, are you dealing with someone who is a salesperson whom you need to guard against?"

The sales culture of the real estate industry creates an atmosphere of distrust.

It should force home buyers who don't want to regret buying their home to be more skeptical of what they are reading or told.

The traditional real estate industry brokerage office encourages in-house sales. An in-house deal involves one or more real estate licensee in the same real estate brokerage. They attempt to "represent" both a buyer and a seller on the same property.

There are obvious conflicts of interest in doing this. The buyer wants the lowest price and best terms. The seller wants the highest price and best terms. The real estate brokerage wants to double-dip commissions. They get a commission from both the list side and buy side of the transaction.

Before the 1980's they did in-house sales at a time when no one represented the buyer. The buyer thought they had an agent but they didn't. Real estate licensees were a seller's agent or a seller's subagent. Neither licensee represented the buyer. With the advent of consumer relationship disclosures buyer representation became an option. Remember, *"one can't serve two masters."* The following are the real estate industry's attempts to keep deals in-house.

Dual agency.

This involves one or more real estate licensees in the same real estate brokerage. They attempt to work with a buyer and a seller on the same property. Disclosed dual agency requires the disclosure that the licensees are providing limited representation. The licensees can't provide certain duties. Undivided Loyalty, Obedience to Lawful Instruction, or Full Disclosure of Material Facts.

Dual agency has an element of "transparency". Transparency requires laying bare the truth. Describing the truth about conflicts of interest is paramount. Exposing and presenting all potential conflicts of interest to both parties is necessary.

The buyer and seller must give their "informed consent". The buyer and seller must understand the consequences of dual agency. They then must give their consent to it. Disclosed dual agency is an acceptable option provided the buyer and seller are aware of what it means.

The buyer is at a disadvantage vs the seller in dual agency. The seller knows what they paid for the property. They know what deferred maintenance there is. They know or suspect what the mechanical issues are. They know what they owe in a mortgage. They have a good idea of what they need to net on a sale of the property. The buyer doesn't know any of this. They can find out what the seller paid for the property. They can estimate what the seller owes on the property. They can get a home inspection. That will help with understanding what deferred maintenance or mechanical issues there are. But the onus is on the buyer to do their due diligence ("Caveat Emptor - Let the Buyer Beware" - Described below).

Is the buyer informed? Is the buyer comfortable with this situation? Then dual agency isn't a major issue. But, in most cases the buyer is the one who will get hurt. Thus, dual agency is not recommended for first time homebuyers in particular. As a result, many states prohibit dual agency. Instead they replace it with one of the below options.

Designated agency.

Designated agency is dual agency but with one big difference. The broker of the company "designates" separate licensees for the buyer and the seller. There are variations of this in different states. But, the usual situation is the designated licensees provide full fiduciary duties.

They now represent the buyer and the seller "without conflicts of interest". Wait a minute. What happened to the conflicts of interest? They are still there, aren't they? Yes, they are still there, but disclosing them is no longer required. The argument is the real estate licensees can operate "independent" of the brokerage. It is like each licensee has their own little brokerage within the real estate company.

But, there is a huge problem with this. Real estate licensees have their license under a managing broker of record. This is the broker who manages the brokerage. It could be the owner of the brokerage. Or, it could be someone hired by the brokerage to act as the managing broker. That broker supervises and oversees the activities of the individual licensees. That broker has responsibility for the licensee's actions. The licensee is not allowed to act "independent" of the brokerage. That is the challenge. Only one state that I know of, Colorado, has regulations that make this possible. All licensees in Colorado are brokers. They may have their license affiliated with a brokerage but they are independent. They are responsible for their own actions. That is not the case in other states with designated agency.

Designated agency is far worse than disclosed dual agency. There is no transparency with designated agency. The truth isn't laid bare. Designated agency hides the truth and deceives buyers and sellers. Conflicts of interest did not go away. They are ignored. But, in some states there might be an upside to designated agency. In some states, such as Massachusetts, designated agency puts the onus on the licensee and brokerage that makes them liable for a breach of fiduciary duties. In other words, they aren't shielded from such liability like happens with transaction brokerage, discussed next. Even though a consumer might have a better chance of suing and being compensated for their loss, it is still a deceptive practice.

Transaction Brokerage.

This option is like dual agency in one regard. Licensees disclose to the buyer and seller that they owe limited representation. In essence the licensees help to process the transaction. Prohibited from favoring one side or the other, they must remain neutral. They can help a buyer make an offer. But they can't suggest a price or terms. They can help a seller understand the details of an offer but they can't suggest a counter-offer.

This option reduces legal liability of the licensees. It also protects their brokerage if sued by a buyer or seller. They aren't "agents". They aren't providing fiduciary duties. Thus, they have a defense against the claim of a breach of fiduciary duty.

The problem of this one is lack of disclosure as I explained about what is happening in Florida. If you had the option of full representation vs using a transaction broker, what would you choose? Most people would choose a true agent and full representation. The cost is same. Real estate licensees aren't paid based on being a true fiduciary vs a salesperson. But if you didn't know you were working with a transaction broker, then you never had a real choice. The traditional real estate industry, at least in Florida, likes it that way.

Facilitator.

This involves full disclosure from the outset that the licensee represents no-one. No limited representation. No deception. Full transparency. Buyer and seller are on their own. Full "Caveat Emptor", Let the Buyer (and seller) Beware!

But, there is a problem with this and other in-house options. Real estate licensees don't know how to operate as a non-agent. They deceive buyers and sellers by calling themselves "agents". They continue to provide advice and suggestions to buyers and sellers. They continue to advertise and market themselves as representing buyers and sellers.

Hence, these in-house deal solutions don't work as they should. Instead, they increase the brokerage's legal liability. The licensees are engaging in what is referred to as "accidental" or "implied" agency. The buyer thinks they have an agent based on the actions and words of a real estate licensee. They then make decisions based on that assumption that they have an agent. Even though the licensee isn't technically their agent, the buyer might be able to prove that they are, based on this concept.

But what buyer or seller is willing to spend the money to sue a brokerage over a loss? Some do, but most don't. Often they don't even know that they incurred a loss. They don't know about the wheeling and dealing that went on behind the scenes. Buyers and sellers get short-changed a lot in these situations. I was having an online discussion with a traditional real estate salesperson recently. I made the point about the dangers for buyers with regard to in-house deals. His response was that, in his experience, it was the seller that usually got short-changed. Like that was OK in his world. Wow!

The best solution is not to get involved in any in-house transaction. Make that known right from the start with any real estate licensee you end up working with.

That leads me to suggest that you adhere to the concept of "let the buyer beware".

"Caveat Emptor" is a neo-Latin phrase meaning "let the buyer beware". It is a principle of contract law in many jurisdictions. It places the onus on the buyer to perform due diligence before buying anything.

This is especially important for a homebuyer. This is due to the lack of *true* representation for homebuyers. The traditional real estate industry focuses on sales, not representation.

As part of this principle, I share the following with you for consideration:

Your real estate "Miranda Warning"!

The Miranda warning, referred to as a person's Miranda rights, is a right to silence warning. Police give it to criminal suspects in police custody before they interrogate them. This preserves the admissibility of their statements against them in criminal proceedings. A Miranda Warning should be mandatory for real estate matters as well.

"You have the right to remain silent. Anything you say, can and will end up used against you! You should not assume that any real estate broker or salesperson represents you. Do not disclose any information you want held in confidence. You should never get involved in or agree to an in-house transaction. Find a licensee who guarantees and pledges to be loyal to you and to be your true agent. This means at all times and in every situation, without exception."

Ask the real estate licensee to sign this pledge and guarantee of loyalty:

A true agent's pledge and guarantee of loyalty.

I hereby guarantee and pledge my undivided loyalty to you. This means at all times and in every situation without exception. I agree not to involve you in any in-house transaction. This is regardless of my state's regulations that say I can do that and still provide undivided loyalty. Such regulations hide and fail to disclose the actual conflicts of interest. I will cancel any agreement with you without penalty in the event of any conflicts of interest. I will refer you to another real estate licensee with a different real estate brokerage, in such case, at your request.

Need Help Finding a True Loyal Agent(R)?

- True Loyal Agents(R) are rare.

- True Loyal Agents(R) have a higher integrity than traditional real estate industry salespeople.

- They have given up one half of a transaction to avoid conflicts of interest.

- Few real estate licensees are willing to do that.

As a result you may not be able to find such an agent in your area on your own.

- They don't brag about their sales.

- They don't display SOLD signs.

Find the best buyer agent in your area.

We can help you.

I have an arrangement with a national buyer agent referral service organization. They help buyers find the best buyer agent to use in their area to help them buy their home. I have worked with this company, the owner, and their staff for more than 28 years.

They provide the third-party oversight. They follow-up and check with both the agents and buyers to see how things are going. They maintain a high level of professionalism at all times.

They are very knowledgeable and supportive of the concept of true buyer representation. They will do their best to find the right agent for you in your area for you to work with.

- They do the interview work for you.

- They know the questions to ask.

- They know the answers they need to hear.

The agent they refer you to might be a True Loyal Agent(R) as I've discussed. If such an agent doesn't exist in your area, they will find a buyer agent they are confident will be able to best serve you. The website is: https://best-buyer-agent-search.com/ There is no cost to you for this service.

Compare this to other agent referral systems. The popular home search portals sell advertising to real estate salespeople. When you want to find an agent, you are referred to those agents who have paid to get referrals. Another popular website, Homelight.com, bases their referrals on the top selling agents. In other words, you get referred to the best salespeople. That is not what you want. None of these websites put any value on true fiduciary representation. Only on sales volume. The referral system that I have set up works much differently. The focus is on true fiduciary representation and not on sales volume. Again, the website to go to is: https://best-buyer-agent-search.com/

Looking on your own for a true buyer agent?

- Make sure that you try to find a smaller, perhaps single office company that doesn't have a lot of licensees. As a result such an office may not have a lot of listings and hopefully none that you would be interested in.

- Look for a licensee who is the broker/owner of the company. They often have more latitude with regard to how they work with a buyer.

- As long as the office agrees to be your buyer agent and not involve you in an in-house deal, you should get decent true representation.

Ask them to sign the true agent's pledge and guarantee of loyalty mentioned earlier.

- Make sure that any buyer agency agreement you sign doesn't include your agreeing in advance to dual agency or designated agency or other form of disloyalty. This is a renege clause which I discuss further below. It allows the brokerage to cancel their true representation in the event you are interested in buying one of their listings. You should cross that section out.

- Should an in-house situation arise make sure they will refer you out to a buyer agent with another company. This is what a true single-party agency would do. They would release you and the new agent you use from any liability for a commission.

Some other items for you to consider:

Agency Disclosures –

Most states have real estate relationship disclosures. You should receive them in a timely fashion. It doesn't help to find out the agent you are using represents the seller after you have signed an offer. They should provide some clarity to real estate consumers, but rarely do. They are often deceptive. They most often are not timely given or often not given at all.

The disclosure describes the types of real estate relationships available in that state. Then, a real estate licensee notes which relationship they intend to have with you.

The Association of Real Estate License Law Officials

ARELLO lists the real estate commissions by state on their website,

https://www.arello.org/resources/regulatory-agencies/#region1

Locate the state you are buying a home in. Click on the state's website for more information specific to your state.

Disclosures aren't Contracts

Generally, a disclosure is not a contract to hire an agent. Signing one shouldn't bind you to that licensee. Most states allow a real estate consumer to refuse to sign a disclosure. In that case, the licensee makes a note that the consumer refused to sign.

You may have to research this further on your own for the state in which you are buying a home. No two states regulations are the same. There is no national standards. The same terminology used by different states often have different meanings.

There is an excellent article about disclosures by the Consumer Federation of America.

https://consumerfed.org/press_release/new-report-real-estate-disclosures-about-agent-representation-often-lack-key-information-are-too-complex-and-are-not-timely/

This was posted on January 13, 2020. "The report – Why Required Real Estate Agent Disclosures About Representation Fail and How They Can Be Improved" – concludes:

"These disclosures are often complex and legalistic, lack important information, are not timely, and are not understood by many home sellers and buyers. The fact that different state disclosure laws use more than 50 different terms to identify seven possible agent roles provides an additional barrier to consumer understanding."

Stephen Brobeck, a senior fellow at CFA and author of the report stated:

"Not knowing whether your real estate agent represents your interests or those of the other party can be costly. An agent working for the other party could, and may be legally required to, pass on compromising information such as the purchase price you're prepared to sell for or spend. And this agent would have no obligation to help you find the right buyer or the right house at the right price."

Exclusive buyer agency agreement –

Such an agreement gives a real estate brokerage the "exclusive right" to be your buyer agent.

Should you sign such an agreement?

It depends. Some agreements are fair and to your advantage. Others trap you into an agreement that isn't in your favor. Often times it depends on who is presenting them to you and what their real intentions are.

I've used them throughout my career. It is important to state the terms of an agreement in writing to avoid misunderstandings.

Generally such agreements are enforceable contracts.

You need to understand what you are signing. If you have doubts, discuss them with an attorney before signing them. I'll review a few of the clauses you should be aware of below.

Don't confuse exclusive buyer agency agreement with exclusive buyer agency.

Exclusive buyer agency is the practice of representing homebuyers only. Exclusive buyer agents never take listings or represent sellers. This definition has prevailed for the past twenty-five years or more. It has the support of authors, two real estate industry's trade associations, and others.

But, the term exclusive buyer agency agreement is now used as a sales tactic. It is a way to confuse homebuyers. The buyer may think they are working with an exclusive buyer agency when they aren't.

What is in the exclusive buyer agency agreement and what should you watch out for?

First, find the "renege clause".

This is the clause that binds you to an in-house deal. You agree in advance to a deceptive, disloyal relationship.

This is where the real estate licensee and the brokerage they are with take back any promise they made to you. They no longer want to be your agent. Instead, they want you to agree, in advance, to ignore conflicts of interest. They want you to let them double-dip commissions at your expense.

Never sign a buyer agent agreement that has such a renege, disloyalty clause in it. Cross it out. If you sign it, you give the licensee the incentive to sell you one of their listings.

A True Loyal Agent(R) would never include such a clause in their agreement. They never get involved in an in-house transaction.

Remember "one can't serve two masters". It doesn't matter what some state regulations claim. Conflicts of interest from an in-house deal don't go away because some regulation says they do.

Second, how long is the agreement for?

Typical is three months for listing and buyer agent agreements. You can always renew the agreement when it expires. Three months is the longest I recommend you agree to. My agreement is a month-to-month agreement. It auto-renews each month until my client buys a home, or either of us decides to cancel the agreement. Anything beyond three months is an attempt to trap you.

Third, look for the "kick-out" clause.

How long is your obligation to pay the brokerage a fee after the agreement ends? There should be some reasonable period of time. This prevents a buyer from taking advantage of a brokerage. But, I've seen such clauses extend that period out for 12 months. The longest you should accept is 30 days. If you agree to a longer period of time it is an attempt to trap you into working with someone you may not want to work with.

Fourth, include a cancellation clause.

You want the ability to cancel in the event that the real estate licensee doesn't meet your expectations. The licensee is favoring showing homes for sale that their brokerage has. The licensee doesn't display the level of professionalism and knowledge you expect. They do this through their words and actions. You should be able to cancel the agreement without further obligation. You may still be subject to the "kick-out" clause but you should have the right to end the relationship. You want to be free to find someone else better suited to your needs.

My agreement is cancellable at any time for any reason without further obligation. As I tell my homebuyer clients.

"Homebuying should be fun and enjoyable. If either you or I don't feel we are working as a team and we are no longer enjoying working together, let's part friends. Either of us can cancel our agreement at any time without further obligation."

Life is too short. If I don't enjoy working with someone, or they don't enjoy working with me, I don't want to continue working with them. Find someone who believes the same. You should not be forced into working with someone you don't trust or like.

Fifth, make sure that you understand what the licensee's compensation is and how it is being paid.

You also need to know if there are any penalties for early cancellation of the agreement. You don't want to get to closing or cancel an agreement and find that you owe the licensee money. It is important for a buyer to discuss upfront how and what to pay their agent. They should include a compensation clause in any written agreement.

Do Buyer Agents Work for Free?

Advertisements claiming that a buyer agent works for free or at no cost are deceptive. Of course, no agent works for free. What the advertisement means is that the agent shares in commissions. Known as co-op offers of compensation, the seller and the listing agent offer these.

If a buyer's agent claims to work for free or at no cost, it means the agent will accept a co-op fee as total compensation. Generally, licensees working with a buyer agree to accept the co-op fee offered to them. Make sure that you know if the licensee is willing to accept the co-op fee in full for their compensation.

There is a problem, in my opinion, with the buyer's agent agreeing to accept the offered co-op fee.

You may not see all properties that may meet your needs. Some listings offer a very low co-op fee or no co-op fee to buyer agents. Many traditional real estate buyer agents review listings by what the co-op fee is first. If it isn't acceptable they throw that listing away even though it might be the most ideal property for the buyer.

This practice has become more widespread with the advent of discount listing companies. Also, some listing agents don't offer a reasonable co-op fee to buyer agents. They want to discourage other agents from showing their listings. This increases their chances of selling the property themselves and double-dipping a commission.

Listing agencies are also taking advantage of the co-op compensation system. They do this through "adverse commission splits".

Most people would guess that the total commission the seller pays gets split 50/50. That hasn't been the case for some time in areas in which I have operated.

The split generally is 67/33 in favor of the listing agency. So a 6% commission goes 4% listing side/2% buying side not 3%/3%. That puts pressure on a buyer agent getting fair compensation. It also creates an interesting situation. I often show my clients 20 to 30 homes. And, often we attempt two or three offers before getting the right home under contract at the right price. How much time do you think a traditional real estate licensee is willing to spend with a buyer? They make twice as much working with sellers?

A better way is for the buyer and the buyer agent to negotiate and agree on compensation.

They agree on the method and the amount in advance. It would include how to handle any differences between that amount and the co-op fee offered. It would include how to handle any incentive bonuses offered.

If the compensation agreement is 2.5% of price paid and the co-op fee was 2%, the buyer would owe the difference at closing.

If the co-op fee offered was 3%, the buyer agent would rebate that difference to the buyer at closing. That way there is no incentive for the buyer agent to show homes based on the compensation offered.

This system does create the potential of the buyer owing extra money to the buyer agent at closing. But, this is included in the negotiation strategy like other closing costs. We know the potential amount that might be due before submitting an offer. So it is easy to take care of such a situation.

Is it a conflict if a buyer's agent compensation is a percentage of the price paid?

No. Real estate agents are generally paid a success fee/commission as a percentage of price paid.

But, you may perceive that it is a conflict of interest. A buyer agent's job is to get you the lowest price. Yet, the higher the price you pay, the higher the commission to the buyer agent.

But, it isn't a conflict of interest. Take a price difference of ten thousand dollars. At a three percent commission—that equals three hundred dollars. It makes no sense to push a buyer client to pay ten thousand dollars more to make an extra three hundred dollars. They know that they would benefit more by saving their buyer client ten thousand dollars. The client would be happy with their service and refer them to others or use their services again in the future.

Will the agent discount the fee?

Don't be afraid to ask prospective agents if they discount or rebate part of their fee back to you. Ask if they offer an alternative compensation model. One such model is paying a retainer and hourly fee instead of a percent of price paid.

Agents working as true fiduciary agents should receive higher compensation than a salesperson. Salespeople don't have the legal obligation to provide fiduciary duties to you. Receiving true fiduciary duties has more value for you.

If an agent is trying to sell you a home you should ask for a rebate. In particular, if they are trying to sell you a home that someone else in the agent's company has listed. After all, the agents are double-dipping the commission.

I have sometimes rebated part of my compensation. I rebate bonuses or overages beyond our agreed-upon compensation. Sometimes a client buys a higher-priced property. If that results in a higher than normal compensation, I will consider a rebate back to my client.

I don't recommend that you make a decision on who to use based on the promise of a rebate.

To get business, some brokerages advertise rebates back to a buyer if you use their services.

The problem with this is that you could save money on the buyer agent fee but end up paying too much for the home. Or buying the wrong home or ending up with a money pit. This could happen if your agent doesn't provide fiduciary duties and undivided loyalty.

True fiduciary agents are specialists. Their focus is on helping you buy the right home at the right price and right terms. Their focus is not on making a sale. If you have a heart condition, you go to a specialist. Do you expect them to discount their fee? Do you think they get paid less than your family physician? Of course not. So be very careful when you are offered a rebate.

Don't get involved in mortgage fraud.

Another potential issue of accepting rebates is mortgage loan fraud. By Marcus Simon, attorney, from the Northern Virginia Association of Realtors website:

https://www.nvar.com/realtors/laws-ethics/legal-blog/debunking-legal-myths-kickback-vs.-rebate

"Many buyer agents have begun to offer to credit a portion of the real estate commission to their clients. It is not illegal (in most states) for an agent to offer to pay money to a purchaser as an inducement to have them sign an exclusive agency agreement. However, this practice can lead to other problems for both purchasers and their agents further down the road, particularly at settlement.

Anytime a purchaser expects to receive a cash credit at closing, it is essential that they make their lender aware of the amount and nature of the credit as soon as possible. The lender will need to adjust the financing appropriately. Failure to do so can easily result in the lender disallowing the payment to the purchaser and possibly causing the entire transaction to unravel.

The biggest problem is that the lender often is not willing to allow cash credits at closing. Most lenders will not allow any escrows, and may limit cash credits to the amount of closing costs actually incurred. Some loan programs do not allow for any closing cost credit. Third party credits, which include a credit from the real estate agent at closing, are often forbidden as well. Underwriters may treat the credit to the purchaser as a reduction in the sales price, affecting the loan to value ratios. Lenders have strict requirements regarding the source of funds of the down payment and the purchaser cash contribution at closing.

In order to make clients happy and "save" the transaction, there may be pressure brought on the settlement agent or the real estate agents to manipulate the numbers on the Closing Disclosure. A real estate agent (and their client) should be very wary of these schemes and avoid being made a party to loan fraud. It is important that the Closing Disclosure settlement statement accurately reflect the entire transaction."

What is the "fee-for-service", compensation model?

In a "fee-for-service", compensation model the homebuyer pays based on services performed. This is different than paying a percentage of the selling price.

This model can take various forms. It can be an "a la carte" price list of services paid based on a particular service or by the hour. It also can combine an hourly fee with a percentage of the selling price. In essence the real estate licensee becomes a consultant. Then the homebuyer and the licensee agree to a set of services and their cost and method of payment.

In the "fee-for-service" model, the homebuyer might pay a retainer fee upfront. Then an hourly fee paid out of the retainer, if there is one, or as billed. At closing, the homebuyer receives a refund of any co-op fee received by the agent, and any retainer fee left over.

The advantage for the agent is receiving compensation for the time expended even if you don't buy a home. This is how we pay most attorneys or consultants.

The advantage to the homebuyer is that you may come out ahead. As long as you buy a home within a short time and don't spend a lot of the agent's time, this might work out.

The contingency fee compensation model, paid as a percent of sale price, puts all the risk on the agent. If a sale doesn't take place, the licensee doesn't receive compensation. The "fee-for-service", "al la carte" model puts the risk on the homebuyer.

The contingency fee model works best for homebuyers short of cash. They may only have enough for the down payment, closing costs, and a contingency/reserve fund.

The retainer/hourly fee model works best for homebuyers who have extra cash. They can pay a retainer, if required, and hourly fees. They have cash for a down payment, closing costs, and a contingency-reserve fund. They also have a good idea of what they want so their agent doesn't spend a long time putting a transaction together.

It also is possible for a homebuyer to combine both compensation models.

They can have their own agent paid on a contingency fee basis. They can have a separate consultant as well paid on a fee-for-service basis as a source of a second opinion.

I have actually done that when I've referred a buyer to another agent out of the area where I operate. The buyer knew me and wanted my advice at various points throughout the process. They felt that having me as a sounding board and a source of a second opinion was helpful. They trusted my advice.

Chapter Seven
Understanding Mortgage Options and Obtaining a True Mortgage Pre-approval

Mortgage professionals assist homebuyers with finding the ideal mortgage program.

They will review your resources: the three C's of homebuying:

- Cash (for down payment and closing costs). Discussed in Chapter Two – Do you have enough cash for a down payment and closing costs?

- Credit (based on your FICO credit score). Discussed in Chapter Three – Do you have credit issues or are your credit scores too low?

- Cash flow (debt to income ratios). Discussed in Chapter Four – Will you be able to find a home you like within your budget?

The combination of cash, credit, and cash flow determines the right mortgage program. This also determines the mortgage amount approval.

It is important for you to know how much you can qualify for and/or be comfortable borrowing. This helps determine the price range of properties you should consider. The difference now is that you are ready to proceed with the "buying phase" of homebuying.

When we discussed mortgages before we were in the "preparation phase" of homebuying. We were getting an idea of what you should be able to afford. We needed to estimate the selling price of a home you would be comfortable with. We then compared that to what your needs were.

We now need to get an actual mortgage pre-approval to continue with buying a home.

Mortgage Programs:

Government-backed programs include those sponsored by the US government.

Federal Housing Administration (FHA):
https://www.hud.gov/buying/loans

Veterans Administration (VA):
https://www.benefits.va.gov/homeloans/

US Department of Agriculture (USDA) rural area loans:
https://www.rd.usda.gov/programs-services/single-family-housing-guaranteed-loan-program

Some states also have their own mortgage programs. With government-backed programs, the government provides a guarantee to the lending institution. This provides an inducement for them to lend money with lower down payments.

Other mortgage programs fall under the category of conventional loans. Each type of conventional loan has unique qualifying requirements. Federal chartered banks and lending institutions must reinvest a part of their funds. These funds must go into low-to moderate-income mortgages in their area of operation. They do this by providing Community Reinvestment Act (CRA) mortgages. Such loans often have lower interest rates and lower down payments. Grants can assist with down payments and closing costs. They have more liberal qualifying requirements than other loans.

Types of Lenders:

- Mortgage brokers. They correspond with dozens of banks and lending institutions. They do not fund a loan. They act as mortgage originators on behalf of a financial institution.

- Mortgage bankers. Mortgage bankers correspond with dozens of banks and lending institutions. They act as the mortgage originators. Mortgage bankers do fund loans. They then resell or assign the loan to another institution or investor.

- Community Banks and Savings and Loan Associations (S&Ls). These are institutions where many people have checking or savings accounts. Banks and S&Ls generally originate, underwrite, and fund loans in-house. But, they often sell your loan to other investors. Yet, even if the bank or S&L sells your loan, it often retains the servicing in-house. That way your payment goes to the bank or S&L that originated your loan. Some smaller banks and S&Ls don't fund or service mortgages as they don't have the resources to do so.

- Credit unions. These are member-owned financial cooperatives. Members control and operate them to promote thrift. They provide credit at competitive rates and other financial services to members. Many people belong to community credit unions. Credit unions offer excellent mortgage and other loan options for their member. These include many not available anywhere else. Credit unions originate, underwrite, fund, and service a loan in-house. But, some smaller credit unions don't have the resources to do in-house mortgages. They often times act like Mortgage Brokers as described above.

Mortgages also come with many payment options:

- The most common is a straight thirty-year fixed rate mortgage. Your monthly payment for principal and interest stays the same for thirty years.

Many lenders also offer a fifteen-year or twenty-year fixed rate mortgage. The payment will be higher as you are paying the loan back in a shorter period of time. But, these will also save you interest.

- Other options include adjustable rate mortgages (known as ARMs). If you know that you plan to stay in a home for three to five years, a 3/1 or 5/1 ARM would be appropriate for your situation. The rate will likely be lower to begin but adjusts after the three-year or five-year term.

Generally, rates go up when the term rolls over. But if you plan to sell and move before the change in rate, you can save money.

But, a decline in the market could make it difficult to sell a home before the rate adjusts. Your home's value may have declined so you can't or don't want to sell. You may end up staying in the home and paying a higher interest rate.

- Another option is to pay points to lower the interest rate. One point is one percent of the mortgage amount. One point on a hundred-thousand-dollar mortgage is one thousand dollars. Your lender can explain and suggest alternatives if appropriate for your situation.

- You should have the option of prepaying your mortgage to save interest and paying it off sooner. Check to make there are no prepayment penalties.

One such option is a "BiWeekly" mortgage payment. This results in your paying one extra month's payment over a year's time. This often shortens the length of time to paying off the loan from thirty to twenty years. This reduces the total interest paid by a lot.

- A twenty-year fixed rate mortgage requires a commitment to a higher mortgage payment. You may want to get a thirty-year fixed rate mortgage and make extra payments from time to time. When you have some extra cash, add some extra money to your regular mortgage payment. Have it apply to principal. Contact the lender to find out the best way to make an extra payment.

If you pay by coupon, sometimes the coupon will have a place to write in the amount of an extra payment. If the coupon doesn't, you should pay the mortgage payment with one check. Then pay the extra amount in a separate check. Add a notation that the extra payment should apply to principal. Otherwise, the lender may apply an extra payment to the escrow account. This is the account used to pay taxes and insurance. If not applied to principal, the payment won't reduce the mortgage balance. It also won't reduce the interest, which is the reason to make an extra payment.

Mortgage Qualifying Letter:

What is a mortgage pre-approval or pre-qualification?

Mortgage pre-approval or pre-qualification certifies your financial viability. A qualifying letter gets issued after you give financial information to a lender. The letter will state the selling price you qualify for and the down payment you plan to make. It will also state the loan program you plan to accept.

Show the letter when you make an offer on a home. This informs the seller and seller's agent that you have met with a prospective lender. It also shows that you qualify for a loan large enough to buy the property. When you agree to buy a home, the seller will take it off the market for from forty-five to sixty days in most cases. This gives the buyer enough time to apply for mortgage financing. The seller and seller's agent don't want to hear forty-five days into the deal that you can't get a mortgage.

Knowing in advance that you pre-qualified reassures the seller and seller's agent. This provides peace of mind, that you will be able to complete the transaction on time.

The Consumer Financial Protection Bureau put lender regulations in place October 3, 2015. Before that the lending community considered pre-qualification the personal opinion of a lender. It estimated what a person would qualify for. But based on information provided by the potential borrower, it wasn't always accurate. The lender did not verify income, employment, assets, or credit.

Pre-approval meant a mortgage commitment. It was subject to having a property under contract. The home had to appraise for at least the selling price. Pre-approval was usually based on a review of a tri-merge credit report and FICO scores. It included verification of employment and income. The borrower provided copies of pay stubs and income tax returns. And, verification of assets with copies of bank and investment account statements. Pre-approval required a more involved, accurate, and reliable process. This was thus more desirable for buyers and potential sellers and their agents.

Since October 3, 2015, the terms pre-qualification and pre-approval mean the same. Some lenders believe that new regulations prohibit them from using the term pre-approval. Today, qualifying letters rarely carry much weight.

There are steps you can take to help your qualifying letter make a good impression.

The lender should verify your financial information. The qualifying letter should state that your financial information was verified. The letter should state something like this, "For this pre-qualification I reviewed a tri-merge credit report and FICO scores. I verified employment and income by means of copies of pay stubs and other documentation. I verified assets by means of copies of bank statements and other documentation."

If the letter doesn't state something similar, the seller may think you don't qualify. Adding the verification language is stronger. If you are competing with other buyers your offer may receive greater consideration.

Meet with several prospective lenders in the beginning. Not to get a qualifying letter but to learn about their mortgage products. Ask lenders about their processes for providing a qualifying letter.

You want a lender who will get a full tri-merge credit report and FICO scores. One who will verify your employment and income with pay stubs and income tax returns. Will they verify your assets?

If the lender doesn't do a thorough review they won't be able to provide you with a strong qualifying letter. I have a local lender who won't do a thorough check. They can only provide what we used to call a pre-qualification. That would leave my clients in a weaker negotiation position. I won't recommend the particular bank due to the policy about qualifying letters. I don't want to put my buyer clients into a weak negotiation position.

If the lender will gather and review information as noted, ask for a copy of the qualifying letter. See what the language says. Ask if the prospective lender will add it to the letter should you decide to seek a loan from them. Many lenders, anxious for your business, will comply. After all, you are asking the lender to put in writing what the lender has verified.

New mortgage regulations do not prohibit lenders from including this language. Still, as a routine practice, lenders don't seem to want to include the language. Ask for inclusion of the language in a qualifying letter—or use another lender who will.

Loan Estimate:

What is a loan estimate and why do you need one?

A rule went into effect on October 3, 2015 that requires borrowers must receive a loan estimate. This is part of regulations overseen by the Consumer Financial Protection Bureau. www.cfpb.gov

The lender provides the official loan estimate on a standardized form. It includes important information. This includes the estimated interest rate, monthly payment, and total closing costs.

The loan estimate gives you information about estimated costs of taxes and insurance. And, how the interest rate and payments may change in the future. The form uses clear language. It's design helps you better understand the terms of the mortgage loan you've applied for.

You must receive a copy of the loan estimate within three business days of applying for a mortgage. The official loan estimate is not used when obtaining a qualifying letter. Instead, a prospective lender should give you an informal estimate of closing costs. This is so you have an idea of what costs and fees are due at closing. This helps with planning.

Find more information on the consumerfinance.gov website:

https://www.consumerfinance.gov/owning-a-home/loan-estimate/

In the "qualifying letter" phase, using one lender is OK.

You only need one letter to make an offer on a home. That changes once you have a home under contract and are ready to make a formal application. I encourage my buyer clients to apply for a mortgage at more than one lender.

As long as you apply around the same time there is no negative impact on your credit scores. Apply for instance to an online lender such as Quicken Loans or Rocket Mortgage. Then to the bank you currently have an account at, and a local mortgage broker. You should develop a list of potential lenders ahead of time. Ask your agent to help you.

Do Not pay any upfront fee. My clients have had negative experiences with some of the online mortgage originators. They attempt to get you to pay a fee upfront in an attempt to "lock you" into using them. If you decide not to go with them it will be very difficult to get that fee back.

Your goal at this point is to have two or three lenders competing for your business. Tell them you are applying at other lenders at the same time and you want their best deal. Then you compare the Loan Estimates from each to see which one is the best to go with.

It helps to have an experienced True Loyal Agent(R) on your side to interpret the results. It is important to compare apples to apples and not apples to oranges. Some lenders may quote a lower rate but a higher processing fee. They also use different names for similar fees which make comparison shopping difficult.

But, my experience is that there can be big variances between loan offers. Skipping this process could be costly. Take you time in comparing the Loan Estimates from each lender. Ask questions if you aren't sure what some aspect of the estimate is about. One of the tools to use in deciding is comparing the APR, the Annual Percentage Rate, discussed next.

Once you have determined which lender you want to go with you give them a "Letter of Intent" to proceed. Then you drop the applications at the other lenders.

Annual Percentage Rate:

What is APR, the annual percentage rate?

Annual percentage rate (APR) is a way of stating the *full* cost a lender charges you for your home loan. APR combines the total amount of interest you must pay plus the cost of other fees and charges that are averaged out over the term of the loan (how long you hold the mortgage).

The various costs rolled into APR can include origination fees, closing costs, broker fees, mortgage points and PMI (private mortgage insurance, if applicable). Generally, APR does not include the cost of an appraisal, title insurance or costs incurred outside of closing.

For that reason, it is important to check what each lender is including in their APR calculations. This is a drawback to using the APR. There is no set standard; lenders include and exclude a range of items. Unfortunately, the Loan Estimate the lender gives you when you apply for a mortgage shows the APR rate but does not list the individual costs that make up that APR. However, to get a correct picture, you need to be comparing APRs calculated on the same basis and including the same costs. So, ask each lender you are considering for the full list of closing costs they are including in their APR calculation.

However, because the APR calculation does take into consideration the closing costs each lender charges, the APR calculation provides a reasonable means by which loans can be compared.

Below, along with general information, you'll find sample calculations that will make understanding APR easier (I hope!). However, not all home buyers are interested in calculating APR or even knowing how it is calculated. That's OK. I happen to enjoy math and numbers, so in case you do also, I've gone into some additional detail.

For those who want to dig deeper, visit my website at: https://make-better-homebuying-decisions.com/ and click on the "Calculate APR" page. I show the exact process of computing APR using a mortgage calculator called *"RECalc"*. You may find this calculator beneficial as you go through the homebuying process. It is available at the Apple App Store.

Comparing APR and different loans from different lenders (or even from the same lender) can be as complicated as you want to make it. You can simply look at the APR and choose the loan that has the lowest number. Or you can spend time calculating various scenarios to arrive at a more perfect decision. Often times the differences are minor and over time don't add up to much.

One of the other drawbacks of putting too much emphasis on APR is that closing costs are averaged out over the term of the loan (for example, 15, 20 or 30 years). But buyers on average, stay in a home just 7 years. Therefore, if you choose a loan with higher closing costs (based on it having the better APR) and you pay off the loan in, say, 5 years, it will probably end up costing you more. Consequently, if you expect to sell and move within 5 to 7 years, take this into consideration before choosing a loan. If you find the calculations too complicated, get lenders to assist you, or ask your Exclusive Buyer Agent or Single-Party Agent to help you decide.

I have also included a link in my resources page for an online APR calculator where you can plug in numbers, hit submit and receive the APR immediately. The APR calculator is at calculator.net:

https://www.calculator.net/apr-calculator.html

For more information about the use of APR check out the bankrate.com website. They have more information about the use of the APR. https://www.bankrate.com/glossary/a/apr/

Let's check out some APR examples.

I have two scenarios to share with you. Scenario One is two loans with the same interest rate but different closing costs. Scenario Two is two loans but with different interest rates and different closing costs.

Scenario One - Two loans with the same interest rate but different closing costs:

Let's assume both loans are $200,000 over 30 years with a 4.5% fixed interest rate. Monthly payment for principal and interest will be $1,013.37 for both loans. However Loan One has $5,745 in closing costs and Loan Two has $9,050 in closing costs. Which is the better deal?

Loan One with closing costs of $5,745 results in a net borrowed amount of $194,255 ($200,000 less closing costs of $5,745 = $194,255 net borrowed). To discover the "effective" interest rate (the APR) we need to take into consideration that you are borrowing less than the $200,000 loan amount. When we recalculate, the payment remains the same. The term of years remains the same.

But the amount being borrowed is lower by the amount of the closing costs you have to pay. In this case the "effective" interest rate (the APR) is 4.75%

Now that we have that rate we can then compare it to the recalculated, effective rate for Loan Two. Loan Two with closing costs of $9,050 means you are borrowing a net amount of $190,950 ($200,000 less closing costs of $9,050 = $190,950 net borrowed). When we recalculate as above with Loan One, the "effective" interest rate is 4.90% for Loan Two.

You can see that when two loans have the same interest rate and monthly payment the decision is easy. You choose the one with the lower closing costs. This is further evidenced by the higher APR for Loan Two and thus Loan Two is more expensive over time.

Scenario Two - Two loans with different interest rates and different closing costs:

Let's assume one loan offered to you has a higher interest rate and monthly payment than the other. Watch here how the loan with the higher interest rate and monthly payment might still cost you less and be the preferred loan.

Let's say Loan One is a $200,000 loan at 4.5% over 30 years, with $9,050 in closing costs (the same as we saw earlier) and a monthly payment of $1,013.37. But Loan Two, in this case, is a $200,000 loan also over 30 years, that carries a slightly higher 4.6% interest rate but has just $3,500 in closing costs and a monthly loan payment of $1,025.29.

Loan One in this scenario has closing costs of $9,050 resulting in a net borrowed amount of $190,950 ($200,000 less closing costs of $9,050 = $190,950 net borrowed). When we recalculate, just as the previous scenario, the "effective" interest rate (the APR) is 4.90%.

Loan Two with closing costs of $3,500 means you are borrowing a net amount of $196,500 ($200,000 less closing costs of $3,500 = $196,500 net borrowed). When we recalculate the "effective" interest rate (the APR) is 4.72%.

So, a little surprisingly, the loan with the higher interest rate and monthly mortgage payment, Loan Two, is in fact the better of the two loans, which is reflected in the lower APR for Loan Two.

Calculating APR and monthly payments like this can get a little unwieldy, unless you enjoy the math. So, be sure to ask your lenders to explain fully and clearly all that you need to know in order to determine your best option. And as I mentioned earlier, your Exclusive Buyer Agent or Single-Party Agent will be happy to help you decide.

Chapter Eight
Looking at All Available Homes

It is vital that you know the local market.

You must develop an intuitive feeling for value.

How do you do that?

See lots of homes for sale.

You shouldn't buy the first home you see, although sometimes it ends up being the best of the bunch. The only way to be sure about the home you decide to buy is to get out and see other similar homes. Also, only by seeing lots of homes will you know what to offer for the home you decide to buy.

Open houses are a great way to get a feel for available homes.

If your price range is up to $175,000, still tour homes up to $200,000. You may come across a home that compares to some you saw priced at $200,000 with an asking price of only $175,000. This could be a sign a motivated seller has priced their home to sell.

A word of caution: The real estate salesperson or seller holding an open house has a goal.

Each wants to find a buyer who falls in love with the home.

A salesperson or seller may ask you personal questions designed to help sell you the home.

Don't give them personal information. You don't want it used against you.

You shouldn't let them know:

- How interested you are in the home.

- How much of a mortgage you qualify for.

- How much money you have for a down payment or where it comes from.

- The price range of homes you are considering.

- Where you work.

- How much you make.

To provide such answers is like playing poker with a mirror behind you. You are allowing others to see your cards. Keep your cards close to your vest at all times but especially at an open house.

- Consider what you wear.

I had a client who was a doctor. She always showed up wearing hospital garb with her stethoscope around her neck. She even had her name badge showing she was a doctor. This telegraphed what she did and, in essence, her financial ability to buy. It made negotiating for a lower price a challenge.

- Watch what you are driving.

If you have a fancy car, leave it at home and take the family van.

- Make sure your agent keeps your finances confidential.

I had another client who had won a large lottery. Real estate salespeople whom she worked with before told sellers she had won the lottery. She couldn't get a good deal no matter how hard she tried until she met with me. I uphold the duty of confidentiality. The seller of the home she bought had no idea where she got her money. That made it easier to negotiate a lower price.

Avoid future annoying sales calls.

If you have followed my advice as noted above you are already working with a True Loyal Agent(R). The agent you are working with should be an exclusive buyer agent or true single-party agent.

Make sure you have their business cards. You need to give them to the seller or the real estate salesperson holding the open house.

Tell the salesperson you have an agent and sign in with your name, but don't give them any contact information.

I have special open house business cards that I give to my buyer clients. The front of the card is the same as my basic business card. But, the back of the card states:

"This Home Buyer Has An Agent. The home buyer handing you this card is represented by the agent noted on the reverse side of this card. Please honor our representation. Do not ask our buyer client for personal, confidential information. Do not ask them to leave their contact information with you. They will leave their name only and give you one of these cards. If they have further interest in the home they will have us contact you. Thank you for your cooperation."

Take the salesperson's business card or seller's contact information. Say if you need further information or have questions, your agent will contact them. Doing so protects your True Loyal Agent(R). It is an ethics violation of the NAR Code of Ethics to contact the "client" of another real estate agent. It also eliminates annoying follow-up sales calls. The open-house agent or seller doesn't have your personal contact information, unless you give it to them. In that case, shame on you!

Start seeing homes:

Besides open houses you are now ready to start seeing homes with the agent you have chosen.

Your agent will set up showings at your convenience to see homes that meet your needs.

If your agent shows you homes that don't meet your needs, ask why you aren't seeing homes more in line with what you want. There may not be any homes in the area that meet your requirements. Then you must discuss what is available. You may have to wait to find something more appropriate. Or, you may have to consider a higher price range or different location.

Staged and Flipped Homes

Staging a home makes it look nice but may hide something. There may be water or pet stains covered with rugs on a hardwood floor. The home may look better with furniture placed by a home staging professional.

Try to imagine your furniture in the home. Look beyond the staging to make sure the layout and condition of the home are satisfactory.

As for flipping, often such homes get cosmetic improvements but little else. They look great but often have hidden flaws. If the home has been recently remodeled, take a closer look. Make sure the owner didn't put "lipstick on a pig," as the saying goes. You should be suspicious of recent remodeling.

Your agent should be able to look up the sales history of the home. They can see when the seller bought it and at what sale price. You can then get an idea of improvements the seller made to the home to see if a price jump is justifiable. If it appears the seller is trying to make a killing and didn't do much, move on to another home.

The physical layout and traffic pattern of a home are also important.

Try to visualize living in the home.

Is it easy to carry groceries from the car to the kitchen? What if the garage is on the opposite end of the home from the kitchen? You would bring groceries through the living room or family room to get to the kitchen.

Think of other such uses of space to make sure a home is livable and meets your physical needs.

Should you consider buying foreclosed homes. Or, HomePath properties, or bank-owned property (REO, Real Estate Owned), or HUD properties?

There is a problem for a first-time homebuyer for such properties. They aren't for the inexperienced buyer. Such properties are more for investors and experienced buyers.

The drawback involves that such properties are generally vacant and need a lot of work.

Utilities are off and offers aren't subject to home inspections. Such homes are generally taken "as is". Many are hard to finance due to their condition, so standard financing is difficult to get. Such homes need special financing.

Make sure you are pre-approved for such a mortgage. Special loan programs allow borrowing money to buy the home as well as an amount to fix it up. FHA 203K is one such mortgage program.

https://www.hud.gov/program_offices/housing/sfh/203k/203k--df

I have helped some buyers go the FHA 203K route. Understand it takes a lot of patience and time to buy such a home. You must have a very cooperative seller. You must be willing to put up with a lot of paperwork and extended time for closing.

Another such program that allows borrowing money to buy a home as well as an amount to fix it up is the Fannie Mae Homestyle Loan.

https://www.lendingtree.com/home/mortgage/complete-guide-to-homestyle-renovation-mortgage/

Here is a good comparison of the two above loan options from Nerdwallet.com.

https://www.nerdwallet.com/article/mortgages/203k-and-homestyle-mortgage-loans-for-home-renovation

My advice to most homebuyers is to stay clear of such properties. You should stay focused on homes in nice condition. You want a home that is easy to resell in five to seven years should you decide to buy another home. Is it something you want to pursue? Make sure the buyer agent you use is familiar with transactions for such a home and can be your guide to making a deal.

Sources of homes for sale.

In most areas, agent listings are in a Multiple Listing System (MLS). MLS systems are usually operated by the local REALTOR(R) Association. All REALTOR(R) members have access to all listings by computer.

But, some properties aren't listed, known as for-sale-by-owner properties.

Make sure your agent shows you as many available homes as possible that appear best to meet your needs. That includes for-sale-by-owner properties if any are available in your area.

Many traditional agents' primary goal is to sell their own or their company's listings. They may direct you to them before showing other listings. They may not want to show you more than six or seven homes, and then they expect you to buy one. They may steer you towards certain listings that offer them higher commissions. And, away from listings that offer a lower commission as discussed before.

They often won't show you for-sale-by-owner properties. They may be uncomfortable or aren't experienced working with for-sale-by-owner properties. Especially when representing a buyer.

In some areas, for-sale-by-owner properties aren't a high percentage of the market. But you should be on the lookout for them.

Make sure you consider enough homes and don't look only at three or four and pick one.

Unless you find the perfect home at the right price.

Exclusive buyer agents and true single-party agents will show you everything available. This includes for-sale-by-owner properties. If you are working with a traditional real estate sales agent, make sure the agent does the same.

Off MLS Listings - Coming Soon, Pocket Listings

Beware of the following tactic used by many traditional real estate industry licensees-salespeople. To entice buyers to work with them, they claim to have off-MLS listings. They say they have pocket listings or coming soon listings. They claim they can offer you an exclusive opportunity to buy them. Such promises are often empty. All listings need to be input into the MLS for all agents to access, as per new MLS regulations.

A seller's best chance of selling for the highest price is to expose it to the entire market through the MLS. They don't want an agent finding a buyer for their home before proper marketing. If an agent does that their focus is on making a deal and double-ending commissions. There is an exception to this. Celebrity sellers often want confidentiality when selling. They might want limited exposure to cut down on curiosity seekers.

Coming soon listings are often used in a hot sellers' market. They create interest in advance of the home being available for viewing. This creates an auction atmosphere and a bidding war. You may want to stay away from such homes. Ask what your agent thinks.

Your agent should also be willing to canvass homeowners.

This is important when there are no homes for sale in a neighborhood that you like.

I canvassed several homeowners on behalf of a client. She loved a particular condo-townhome project and wanted to live there. We saw several for sale, but she wanted an end unit with a particular view. I identified a dozen that would meet her needs. I then mailed out a letter to the owners indicating that I had a buyer client interested in their property. I had three owners who responded saying they would sell. I ended up putting a deal together on one at a very good price for my buyer client.

In my experience, exclusive buyer agents and single-party agents have more flexibility.

They seem to have more desire to find the right property for their buyer clients. They think outside of the box to help their buyer clients find and buy a suitable home. They aren't "in a hurry" to make a sale. The "in a hurry" to make a sale is the salesperson mindset. Avoid that.

Property Tax Exemptions: Do You Qualify?

I am including this section on property tax exemptions for two reasons.

First, does the current owner have any property tax exemptions? Get a copy of the latest property tax bill for any home you are considering buying. You, or your agent, can get this from the local tax assessor.

Examine it for tax exemptions. Are you eligible for the same exemptions or will they go away when you buy the home? In which case your real estate taxes may go up in the near future. You should be aware of this when estimating your monthly expenses. If you are escrowing taxes in your mortgage payment, your monthly mortgage payment will also increase in the future.

Second, whether the current owner is taking advantage of any tax exemptions, are there any that you might be eligible for. These could reduce your property taxes in the future. This would result in a reduction also of your mortgage payment if you are escrowing taxes.

From houselogic.com:

https://www.houselogic.com/finances-taxes/taxes/property-tax-exemptions/

"You may qualify for a money-saving property tax exemption. Here's the thing. The state, county, or city agency that collects your property taxes usually won't tell you that you qualify for an exemption. You need to find and apply for property tax exemptions offered in your area. Check the websites of tax agencies in your area to find out what tax relief is available. Nobody likes paying a dime extra in taxes. But when it comes to property taxes, you could pay too much if you don't know you qualify for an exemption. You might spend a few hours doing the research and the paperwork, but you could lower your tax bill enough to make it worth your time."

Here are five of the most common types of property tax exemptions.

- Homestead:

Homestead exemptions keep you from paying tax on a portion of your home value.

- Seniors and The Disabled:

Many states offer property tax exemptions to older homeowners and the disabled.

- Military Veterans:

Many states offer property tax exemptions to veterans if they: use the home as their primary residence; served during wartime and were honorably discharged. Some states offer property tax exemptions to all veterans, even those who served during peacetime.

- Renovations:

If you make home improvements, check for property tax breaks. Generally if you make improvements that add value to your home the assessed value for tax purposes will go up. As a result your property taxes will increase in the future. Some renovations are exempt from this process.

- Energy Incentives:

Installing renewable energy systems in your house could pay off on your property tax bill as well as your energy bill. Some states exclude the value of certain green improvements from a home's real estate assessment. Eligible upgrades may include the installation of solar panels or geothermal heat pumps.

- Other Exemptions:

A visit to your local tax assessor's office may turn up other less common property tax exemptions. For example, some communities exempt property you build or renovate to give a grandparent a home. Some reduce the assessed value of the homes of volunteer firefighters. Others might offer widow/widower exemptions.

Property Tax Appeals. Are your property taxes too high?

While we are on the topic of real estate taxes, let me bring up one more thought. Real estate taxes are supposed to provide an equitable method for home owners to finance local government operation and services. However, the system is fraught with the potential for some homeowners paying far more than their share and others to pay less. If you are in the paying far more category, you should consider challenging your assessment and getting your property taxes lowered.

I have experience in this. I would examine a buyer client's taxes to see if they are reasonable based on the price they paid for their home. When it was obvious that they were overpaying I would help them challenge their taxes.

Forbes has an excellent article on challenging property taxes.

https://www.forbes.com/sites/johnwasik/2018/07/13/how-you-can-save-money-by-appealing-your-property-tax-assessment/#c48836c75fcc

"Millions of homeowners have no idea they can actually lower their property taxes. They casually glance -- or grimace -- at their mortgage escrow notice every year and pony up without doing a thing. Despite possible savings of thousands of dollars, only 2% of homeowners appeal their assessments, which is the first step in lowering taxes. And here's an even bigger disconnect: Some 60% of properties are overvalued by assessors, according to the National Taxpayers Union."

One of my clients and I started a business doing property tax appeals in the Albany, NY area. Our average annual property tax savings for our clients is $2000, with some as high as $5000 annual savings. Yes, you can challenge your own taxes in your local area, but if there is a reputable service locally that challenges property taxes on homeowner's behalf, consider it.

Our experience is that local assessors started trusting us to do a good job for our homeowner clients. As a result we were able to obtain tax reductions that the homeowner couldn't get on their own. The assessors were well aware of our skills at maneuvering the system and challenging them in a manner that would stick in court. As a result our outcomes were successful. We often represented homeowners who appealed their taxes themselves the previous year and lost. It is rare that we don't get a substantial property tax reduction the following year.

Challenging tax assessments takes skills and knowledge that most people don't have or don't want to learn. As a result homeowners are often frustrated with the system and the results. If you are willing to take the time to understand the system and challenge your property taxes yourself, by all means, do it. If, on the other hand, you don't want to take the time to learn the process or to challenge your property taxes on your own, then find someone to do it for you. Yes, it will cost you to hire someone to do it. But, the savings are annual and you will benefit long-term.

You should be able to find a professional property tax agent locally. Search for "property tax appeals" and your local municipality. Some real estate licensees and attorneys offer such a service as well. Ask them to provide examples of their work. What savings have then been able to get for other clients? What do they charge and how is it paid? What references can they provide you?

Chapter Nine
Developing a Negotiating Strategy
Before Making an Offer

Home buyers often talk about "submitting a bid" as if buying a home was an auction.

Yes, you can buy a home at an auction. HUD homes are an example. Bank owned property is often sold that way. But the usual process of buying a home differs from that.

Serious consideration is needed when submitting an offer to buy.

The three parts of developing a negotiation strategy.

- What price?

- What terms?

- What contingencies?

If you want the best outcome for your homebuying adventure, develop a negotiating strategy before making an offer.

Making an offer to buy real estate will vary between states and even within the same state.

Some areas use a two-step process. Step one is a simplified "offer to buy" contract. It lists most of the terms, conditions, and contingencies that the buyer and seller agree to. It acts like a memorandum of a final agreement. Step two is a more formal contract and includes lots of legalese. This is then signed later, after home inspections and further negotiations.

In other areas the buyer and seller sign a formal contract at the beginning.

Ask your agent which forms they use or prefer and what the local procedures are.

Should you use an attorney?

As these are legal contracts my advice is to have legal counsel review the contract. They should do this before you sign. Or, after you have signed making the contract subject to your legal counsel's review and approval.

Be aware that in some areas attorneys don't play a big role in the homebuying process. In these areas, real estate agents take on a larger role. And closings often take place at title companies and not at attorney offices.

But, buying a home is one of the largest financial transactions that you are likely to make in your lifetime. You should not make this without an experienced real estate attorney by your side. Buying a home has a multitude of complex issues involved in the process.

Most attorneys feel that they can do a real estate closing whether that is their specialty or not. I've had clients use attorneys who handled a divorce or estate settlement. They had no real estate experience. These closings were disasters. If you are going to use an attorney, please do yourself a favor. Use one who does real estate closings as a routine part of their practice.

An experienced real estate attorney will take the confusion out of the transaction. They will take the time to explain the process while keeping you informed every step of the way. They can give advice on all legal aspects of the real estate transaction. This is from the initial offer, the negotiation of the contract and the closing.

An attorney can help you decide how to take title. They handle and oversee the consummation or closing process. Buying a home should be a rewarding experience, not a painful one. The right attorney can make the conveyance as simple and as painless as possible for the client.

Knowing what to expect and how to prepare for the closing can help cut stress. This will result in a pleasant experience. Find an attorney who understands how important this transaction is to you. Will they commit to preparing you for this final step in your transaction?

Price Considerations When Making an Offer:

Find a starting point.

Rules of thumb such as starting at ten percent off list price generally don't work. Some homes are fifteen to twenty percent overpriced. Other prices are on the money or below market value.

In some tight markets, paying above list price is often necessary. This is due to a limited number of quality homes or condos for sale. Along with a large number of buyers who want to buy a home or condo in those areas.

Regardless of the market situation, set the highest price you would pay for the property. Then start at a price below that limit that is still supported by facts. What is the home's condition? What is the selling prices of other similar homes? Does the starting price still allow for negotiation room with the seller?

Try to avoid a bidding war if that is what transpires at the time you are buying.

Some homes sell way above what they are worth. Such a market isn't sustainable, and many buyers will regret overpaying for their homes. Buyers overpaid from 2007 to 2009. Similar conditions are appearing currently in some areas of the country. If you are in competition with other buyers, you generally have one chance. You must present your best offer or risk having no chance. That might lead to your overpaying. Discuss this with your agent. But, don't get too carried away.

Thirteen Tips for determining a starting offer price.

- What did the seller pay for the property?

Did the seller recently buy the property? Are they asking a lot more for it now? Did they do anything to it to improve its value? You should know so that you may be able to negotiate a better price, since the seller may have some cushion to work with.

- What does the seller owe on the property?

It is possible to check at the local clerk's office for copies of recorded deeds and mortgages. In most areas this information is available online.

See if a mortgage is outstanding on the property. Compare the amount of mortgage against the sale price. This will help determine an approximate amount of equity the seller might have in the home. The greater the equity, the greater the potential that the seller has some room in the price to work with.

Say a seller paid $200,000 and took out an FHA mortgage for $205,000 three years ago. Chances are the seller has very little room to negotiate. The asking price might be very close to the seller's breakeven point. Besides the mortgage, the seller has closing costs and commissions to pay.

- How long has the seller owned the property?

If the seller has owned the property for a very short time you should get an idea about why they are selling so soon.

- Is this a property flip?

Has an investor bought the property and done cosmetic improvements?. Are they now looking to make a large profit?

- Was the property inherited?

Heirs often times have no interest in moving into the property nor spending any time or money fixing it up. They may be very interested in getting rid of the property at a below market price for a quick sale.

- Does it appear the seller actually lived in the property?

You may have decided to buy an investor-owned property. How well was the property maintained? Owner-occupants seem to take care of their property better than investors or tenants.

- What improvements has the seller done since owning the property?

What is the value of the improvements? Is there some cushion in the seller's asking price? This might give you better negotiating leverage. You should have a sense of what they did to the property and what they may have invested.

- What are similar homes selling for in the area?

Your agent should run a comparative market analysis (CMA) of similar homes sold and on the market. You should know the market value of the house you want to buy and whether it is in line or out of step with the asking price. You should have hard evidence to support your offering price. Especially if it is lower than asking price in order for your offer to be credible.

Real estate salespeople will show you the higher end of comparable homes. Their goal is to encourage a higher offering price. Your agent should show you a wider range of sold homes. That way you see that some homes sell well below the asking price for the home you are considering.

- What is the home worth to you?

Market data is one thing, but an intuitive feeling is another. What other homes have sold for and the asking price of other homes on the market offer a guide. But what if the home is perfect for you or has features important to you?

The home may be worth more to you than to other buyers. Take such considerations into account in determining what the home is worth to you. Are you willing to pay more for the home, even if it exceeds the market data valuation?

I recently had two clients find the perfect homes. Both had asking prices higher than the market indicated. I told them I couldn't justify the price they would have to pay. But my clients decided to go ahead anyway as each property was ideal in their mind.

One client was paying cash so an appraisal for a mortgage wasn't a concern. But, the other client was getting a mortgage and that raised a concern. When homebuyers get a mortgage, the home must appraise for the sale price or higher. Lenders base a mortgage on the lower of the appraised amount or sale price. If it appraised less my client would have to come up with more cash down payment to make up the difference. Whew, it appraised for the selling price.

- What defects or potential defects does the home have?

You should make your offer subject to a home inspection. You need to make sure you aren't buying a money pit.

- Is there deferred maintenance?

I always look for a service record on the furnace. It is prudent to have a furnace cleaned every year. Especially for an oil-fired furnace or boiler. If there is no service record on it I look to see if it appears dirty. If it is dirty and no service record, I suspect the rest of the home isn't cared for either. An unmaintained furnace should be a warning to check other mechanical systems also.

Oil-fired boilers or furnaces require annual maintenance. Heating oil is not flammable as is. It has to be atomized by forcing the oil through small nozzles to create a mist. These nozzles get gummed up and need replacement annually.

- How is the neighborhood? Crime? Noise? Smells? Ease of access?

You are the one who is going to live there. If you want to know how the neighborhood is, visit at different times of the day. Call the local police department to ask about crime rates in the area. Drive by with the windows down. See if there are any loud noises or obnoxious smells coming from an industry or farm close by. Check on where the nearest airport is and what the flight paths are.

- Concerned about sex-offenders?

Most states have a sex-offender registry. Google, "sex-offender registry" for your state. Ask your agent if they know where you can check by entering the address of potential homes.

- What about low-balling?

If the seller senses you are making a low-ball offer, the seller won't take your offer as serious. They may not counter it. Is the seller put off by your actions? They may not consider a reasonable offer from you later.

Low-balling is in the eyes of the recipient. You may not consider your offer a low-ball offer, but the seller might. It helps to have some data and support for your offer so that it appears to be reasonable.

When determining a negotiating strategy, price isn't everything.

Take into consideration your strengths and the strength of your offer.

- You should have as strong a qualifying letter from a lender as possible.

You will make your offer subject to obtaining financing on the terms you need. You should provide the seller and the seller's agent with a strong qualifying letter. It should state that it included a review and verification of your credit, income, and assets.

Determine how much of the information on the qualifying letter you want to share. The seller and the seller's agent want to know if you qualify to pay the list price. Say you qualify, for example, up to a $250,000 price. If making an offer on a home with a $220,000 asking price, how do you present the qualifying letter to the seller and agent? Do you black out the $250,000 figure and state that your qualification is enough for the price you are offering? Or do you show the actual qualifying sale price?

The seller may counter at a higher price if they and their agent know the price you qualify for. If the seller believes you want the home they then know you can afford to pay more. But, showing that you qualify for more than what you are offering shows strength. Have you predetermined the highest price you are willing to pay? Are you willing to stick to it? Then showing the qualified loan amount may work in your favor. This is especially if you are competing with other offers. Discuss the strategy with your agent. Determine how the agent feels about it and what the agent recommends.

- Can you offer a quick closing?

If you are paying cash that would be the case. If you are pre-approved for a mortgage it might also be the case. Being pre-approved could mean reduced delays in closing. If this is the case a seller may give your offer greater consideration at a lower price. Especially if they have a strong need for a quick close and you are able to accommodate them.

- Can you delay closing?

What if the seller has a need to delay the closing? If they are building a new home they may need more time before they are ready to move, to avoid a double move. Try to arrange for a longer mortgage commitment as long as it doesn't cost you extra. If you have no problem with the extended timing of the closing this might work to your advantage. You may even be able to negotiate a lower price.

- Can you delay moving in after closing?

Another option seller's sometimes would like, is to stay in the home after closing for 30 to 45 days. They may need the money from closing to buy their next home, but they need extra time to move. Or, they would like some time in which to paint and improve the home they are buying before having to move. In such a case they enter into a written agreement with you approved by your attorney. They prepay you rent at closing for the period you both agree to. They also pay a security deposit in the event they don't move out when they should.

Consider the seller's motivation to sell.

Take advantage of these seven seller motivations.

- Is the home vacant or soon to be?

- Is the seller concerned about vandalism or carrying costs?

They may be willing to sell at a reduced price.

- Have the sellers purchased another home?

Do they have another home under contract subject to selling the home you want to buy? The seller may be carrying the costs of maintaining two homes. The seller may be very interested and motivated for a quick sale at a reduced price.

- Has the property been on the market for a long time?

Check for expired listings with the current agent or previous agents. The seller may have been more optimistic about their selling price then they should have. The seller may be ready to deal now.

- Are the owners divorcing?

When walking through the home, look for signs of a separation or divorce. Does it appear that someone has moved out?

- Is the property in foreclosure?

Often you can buy a property in foreclosure in a short sale. What if the market value of a home is less than what the owner owes on the mortgage? A lender may accept less than the loan amount due, because doing so is preferable to foreclosing on a loan. Hence the term "short sale". The lender receives less than the amount owed.

Beware that although it makes financial sense for a lender to agree to a short sale, they don't act like it. They often drag out a decision for months. Generally, a short sale isn't the best route for a first-time homebuyer.

But, if the home is in foreclosure and the seller has equity in the home, it may be worth pursuing. It is possible that the seller will consider a lower price rather than lose the home and equity later.

- Has a death or illness in the family forced a sale?

Often someone inheriting a home has no interest in owning it and wants a quick sale to settle an estate. Knowing about a death, illness, or inheritance can help with the negotiating process.

Other negotiating considerations include:

- What is the likely counter-offer from the seller?

Try to envision different counters from the seller. The seller can reject your offer, accept it, or counter it with changes, generally in the price.

- What will be the amount of your next counter-offer?

Congratulations if you were able to start at a price below what you feel the home is worth. You now may have room to move once you have an idea of the seller's potential flexibility.

- Should you ask for a closing cost credit, also referred to as a seller concession?

Many loan programs allow for a seller to help with a buyer's closing costs. Seller concessions generally range between three and six percent of sale price.

But, the seller may not be providing a concession, as the name implies. Rather the seller is providing a way for you to finance in some of your closing costs. I provided an example of this before, but it is worth repeating.

Say the seller is asking $200,000 but would take $190,000. You would like the seller to help out with your closing costs and ask the seller to pay $8,000. You offer $190,000, with an understood net price to the seller of $182,000. But the seller, wanting $190,000, counter-offers at $198,000. Then paying $8,000 toward your closing costs the seller nets $190,000.

Who paid the $8,000? In this case, you did. Your sale price may have increased by $8,000 over what you may have paid for the home without the concession. Use seller concessions for closing costs if necessary. Keep them toward the lower end of allowed amounts. It may be better to find money somewhere else then to increase the sale price and mortgage.

Some loan programs include a bank-provided closing cost credit. Such programs will end up with a higher interest rate to offset the cost of the credit. This may be better than using the closing cost credit noted above.

- How do you handle repair issues?

Should you ask the seller to make certain repairs? Should you ask for a repair credit or offer a lower price and handle repairs yourself?

If you ask the seller to make repairs, are the repairs done in a good workmanlike manner?

The seller may complete repairs or get a neighbor to help out. The seller nor the neighbor may have adequate skills or experience to do repairs well.

I recommend getting a repair credit at closing or reducing the price. The buyer then makes repairs by hiring tradespeople suitable to the buyer. Are the intended repairs major or minor? Is the bank appraisal requiring them before closing. If the appraisal comes up with repairs or if the repairs are major, the lender may not allow a repair credit. They may need those repairs made before closing or may hold money in escrow pending repairs.

A buyer and seller might negotiate repair credits between themselves for closing. But often closing documentation must show details about repair credits. That could bring scrutiny by the lender about the extent of repairs to take place. One way to handle this is by using the seller concession for closing costs. Instead of asking for a repair credit ask for a closing cost credit. That way you can use the money you had reserved for closing costs, that the seller is now paying, for repairs. Discuss the matter of repair credits with your agent and your attorney.

- What can you give up in negotiating that isn't as important to you as it may be to the seller?

Sometimes it makes sense to ask for things in your initial offer that aren't important to you. You then can use them later in negotiating as a give-back to the seller. An example may be asking for the washer and dryer. Washers and dryers seem to be personal to some people.

Ask for the seller to include the washer and dryer. Then when the seller asks for them back use it as a negotiation tool to get a better price. You may have your own washer and dryer or want to buy new ones, so such a tactic may work well for you.

Successful negotiating is a complex process.

You should be aware of the nuances of negotiating to get the best price and terms.

A strength of a good buyer agent is the experience of negotiating on behalf of buyer clients every day. They have developed excellent negotiation knowledge and techniques. This helps their buyer clients achieve success in the homebuying process.

Before you sign an initial contract to buy real estate, do your homework.

- **Develop a strategy.**

- **Seek help.**

- **Don't be afraid to walk away if the seller refuses to meet your price and terms.** You may still be able to buy the home at your price and terms if the seller softens up a bit and no other offers come in.

One buyer client of mine made an offer once a month for four months on a home. We reduced the price with every offer. The seller accepted the fourth offer at a much lower price than their initial offer. My client got a great deal on the home by waiting out the seller, a relocation company.

- **Be patient, and you too may end up with a great deal on a home.**

Chapter Ten
Including Contingencies for
Property Inspections

Know the home you are buying.

You can start with an informal idea of the condition of a home before making an offer.

Do you know someone knowledgeable about building structural components and mechanical systems? Go through the home with them before writing an offer to buy it. By doing so, you will have information to help determine your negotiating strategy.

This could be a relative, a contractor, or your real estate agent. Get information in the form of personal opinions without it costing you money. Make sure the person you rely on is knowledgeable about property evaluations.

A word of caution. A licensee, unless they are your fiduciary agent, may not be looking out for your best interest. Only rely on the opinion of an agent if that agent is acting as your agent. Do they have the experience, knowledge, and background to produce a valuable opinion? Make sure they do.

For example, I have over 45 years of real estate experience. I've attended thousands of home inspections. My experience provides my clients with an excellent idea of the general condition of a home. I'm able to provide this when we first take a look at a home. My client is getting a feel for whether the home meets with their ideal. I'm looking at the mechanical and structural aspects of the home. I point out obvious situations of concern. These might either rule out the home or at least provide the buyer with areas of concern to look into further.

Property Condition Disclosures.

In some states, sellers must disclose known defects. They may provide you with a seller's property disclosure. In other states, that isn't required.

But, in most states agents have to disclose known defects in a property. Yet, many agents don't investigate the condition of property they list. They don't want to know about issues. If they did, they would have to tell prospective buyers abut such problems.

I've had situations where I've found obvious defects in a property. I discussed them with the listing agent only to have the agent deny the defects and not take any action on them. They resented that I even brought them up. It would make it more difficult to sell a home disclosing defects. It was unethical and illegal in many situations for the agent not to disclose the defects.

I had one situation whereby my client cancelled a contract due to the inspection results. The seller's unwillingness to deal with the health and safety issues left us no choice. The home had deteriorated asbestos wrap on heating pipes in the basement. It also had major unsafe electrical issues including "knob and tube" wiring in the home.

Asbestos Hazards:

Asbestos refers to a group of mineral fibers found in rock. For decades, asbestos had a use as a building material in homes and other buildings. Asbestos is usually white, and its matted fibers can be crumbly if deteriorated.

Asbestos is no longer often used in commercial applications. But it is still found in many older homes and buildings. You may find asbestos wrapped around older hot water pipes and water boilers. Or, used to tape together sections of heating ducts. Most of the time asbestos poses very little risk to your health. The fibers are only a risk if they release into the air and inhaled.

Inhaled asbestos fibers can become lodged in your lungs and remain there. This can cause scarring and inflammation. Exposure to high concentrations of asbestos in the air can be harmful to your health. It can increase your risk of getting a variety of diseases. These include asbestosis (scarring of the lungs); lung cancer; and mesothelioma. Mesothelioma is a rare form of cancer of the lining of the body cavity.

Knob and Tube Wiring Hazards:

Knob-and-tube wiring is an early standardized method of electrical wiring in buildings. It was in common use in North America from about 1880 to the 1930s. It is unsafe and holds the potential to start house fires. You should remove it from use. Then replace it with electrical wiring that meets current codes.

The agent and the seller were well-aware of the issues. We provided them with a copy of the inspection report for their information. Once we cancelled the contract the seller needed to update the property disclosure. The seller did not. The home sold to another buyer and I inquired with them whether they knew about the hazards. They were not told. This was an illegal act by the seller and an unethical act by the real estate licensee.

Remember my discussion on "Caveat Emptor", let the buyer beware. As a buyer, you should ask for the seller to fill out and sign a seller's statement of property condition. It doesn't matter if required or not. You may encounter resistance to the request. It doesn't mean that the seller wants to hide something. It is more an issue of legal liability. Sellers often fail to disclose something or make mistakes providing the information. That increases their legal liability to you. Not providing the form removes potential liability.

A good negotiating tool is to ask for a seller's statement of property condition. Then drop your request during negotiations. This gives you leverage toward getting something else more important to you.

If a seller provides such a disclosure, it is not a substitute for property inspections. Problems may exist in the home that the seller doesn't know about. Or, they may not list items on the disclosure through ignorance or a weak memory. Real estate licensees do not to help a seller fill the form out. It increases their liability to any buyers if they do.

"For Your Protection: Get a Home Inspection."

This is the title of a document from HUD, the Department of Housing & Urban Development, For Your Protection: Get a Home Inspection.

https://documentcloud.adobe.com/link/review?uri=urn:aaid:scds:US:6be1b128-1788-470b-8105-71c8032cc055

HUD requires buyers to sign if they are getting an FHA mortgage. Ask your agent or lender for a copy or review one at the link above.

From the document:

"You must make a choice on getting a Home Inspection. It is not done for you. You have the right to examine your potential new home with a professional home inspector. But a home inspection is not required by law and will occur only if you ask for one and make the arrangements. You may schedule the inspection for before or after signing your contract. You may be able to negotiate with the seller. You may want to make the contract contingent on the results of the inspection. For this reason, it is usually in your best interest to conduct your home inspection as soon as possible. A professional home inspector takes an in-depth, unbiased look at your potential home. They check the physical condition. Things like the structure, construction, and mechanical systems. They identify items that need repair. They estimate the remaining useful life of major systems, equipment, structure, and finishes."

HUD also has a list of ten questions to ask home inspectors:

1. What does your inspection cover?

They should ensure their inspection and report will meet all applicable state requirements. They should follow a well-recognized standard of practice and code of ethics. You should be able to request and see a copy of these items ahead of time and ask any questions you may have. If there are any areas you want to make sure they inspect, be sure to identify them upfront.

You should also ask what items they don't cover or inspect. Some inspectors will inspect alternative heating systems. Others won't. Some do termite inspections and others don't.

Ask if the inspector will share his observations with you while at the home. Will they allow you to follow them around and ask questions? No question is stupid. You don't know what you don't know. This is your inspection. You are paying for it. I've had inspectors tell buyers to sit in the kitchen and wait. He would meet with them later to tell them what he found. That is unacceptable. Make sure they are OK with you staying with them and asking questions during the inspection.

2. How long have you been practicing in the home inspection profession?

How many inspections have you completed?

The inspector should be able to provide his or her history in the profession. They may be able to provide a few names as referrals. Newer inspectors can be very qualified, and many work with a partner. Or they may have access to more experienced inspectors to assist them in the inspection.

3. Are you experienced in residential inspection?

Related experience in construction or engineering is helpful. But this is no substitute for training and experience in residential home inspections. If the inspection is for a commercial property, then ask about that as well.

4. Do you offer to do repairs or improvements based on the inspection?

Some inspector associations and state regulations allow the inspector to perform repair work. Other associations and regulations forbid this as a conflict of interest.

5. How long will the inspection take?

The average on-site inspection time for a single inspector is two to three hours. This is for a typical single family house. Anything less may not be enough time to perform a thorough inspection.

6. How much will it cost?

Costs vary depending on the region, size and age of the house, scope of services and other factors. A typical range might be $300-$500. But consider the value of the home inspection based on the investment you are making. Cost may not reflect quality. HUD does not regulate home inspection fees.

7. What type of inspection report do you provide and how long will it take to receive the report?

Ask to see samples. Determine whether you can understand the inspector's reporting style. Do the time parameters fulfill your needs. Most inspectors provide their full report within 24 hours of the inspection.

The best reports are computer generated with photos and detail descriptions. The first 5 to 8 pages provide a summary of key issues that the inspector found that need further scrutiny. This is the part of the report shared with the seller to negotiate repairs. Then the rest of the report provides details of other observations. Some inspectors use a check box form with no photos or specifics. Others write up a summary with very little detail and few photos. These are unacceptable and aren't helpful.

8. Will I be able to attend the inspection?

This is a valuable educational opportunity. An inspector's refusal to allow this should raise a red flag. Never pass up this opportunity to see your prospective home through the eyes of an expert.

This to me is the most important aspect of buying a home. You spent 20 to 45 minutes at the first visit to the home. You now have 2 to 3 hours to get to know the home. You have the opportunity to find out if there are problems with the home. Are any issues cause to cancel the contract? If the seller will help repair the issues are you still willing to buy the home? Do you still like the flow of the home and does it still meet your needs?

9. Do you maintain membership in a professional home inspector association?

There are many state and national associations for home inspectors.

There are two national home inspector associations:

The American Society of Home Inspectors, ASHI. https://www.homeinspector.org/

The National Association of Certified Home Inspectors, NACHI. https://www.nachi.org/blind.htm

10. Do you take part in continuing education programs.

Do you keep your expertise up to date? A commitment to continuing education is a good measure of their professionalism. This is especially important where the home is older or includes unique elements.   These need extra or updated training.

Include a contingency in your offer to buy a home for home inspections.

Your offer should be subject to you paying for a home inspection and other testing. The offer is subject to the results being satisfactory to you. If they aren't you can cancel the contract and receive your deposit back.

The extent of such a general inspection depends on the home you want to buy.

Ten inspections and tests that aren't included in most general home inspections:

- **Radon Testing:** https://www.epa.gov/radon.

From the EPA, Citizen's Guide to Radon:

"Radon is a cancer-causing, radioactive gas. You can't see radon. And you can't smell it or taste it. But it may be a problem in your home.

Radon causes many thousands of deaths each year. That's because when you breathe air containing radon, you can get lung cancer. The Surgeon General has warned that radon is the second leading cause of lung cancer in the US today. Only smoking causes more lung cancer deaths. If you smoke and your home has high radon levels, your risk of lung cancer is especially high.

Radon occurs all over the United States. Radon comes from the natural (radioactive) breakdown of uranium in soil, rock and water. It gets into the air you breathe. Radon can get into any type of building—homes, offices, and schools—and result in a high indoor radon level. But you and your family are most likely to get your greatest exposure at home, where you spend most of your time.

You should test for radon. Testing is the only way to know if you and your family are at risk from radon. EPA and the Surgeon General recommend testing all homes below the third floor for radon.

You can fix a radon problem. Radon reduction systems work, and they are not too costly. Some radon reduction systems can reduce radon levels in your home by up to 99%. Even very high levels are reducible to acceptable levels."

- Lead Paint Testing: https://www.epa.gov/lead.

From the EPA.gov website:

"For homes built before 1978, there is a good chance it has lead-based paint. In 1978, the federal government banned consumer uses of lead-containing paint. Some states banned it even earlier.

Lead from paint is one of the most common causes of lead poisoning. This includes lead-contaminated dust. Lead paint is still present in millions of homes, sometimes under layers of newer paint. If the paint is in good shape, the lead paint is usually not a problem.

Deteriorating lead-based paint (peeling, chipping, chalking, cracking, damaged, or damp) is a hazard. It needs immediate attention. It may also be a hazard when found on surfaces that children can chew or that get a lot of wear-and-tear. Including windows and windowsills, doors and door frames, stairs, railings, banisters, and porches.

Be sure to keep all paint in excellent shape and clean up dust often. Lead in household dust results from indoor sources such as deteriorating lead-based paint. Lead dust can enter a home from soil outside due to exterior lead-based paint issues.

Renovation, repair, or painting activities can create toxic lead dust. This happens by disturbing or demolishing painted surfaces containing lead paint. Learn more about hiring lead-safe certified contractors."

For more information - www.epa.gov/lead, on the right-hand side under Popular Links is a link to the EPA pamphlet, "Protect Your Family from Lead in Your Home".

https://www.epa.gov/lead/protect-your-family-lead-your-home-real-estate-disclosure

Lead poisoning is the nation's number one environmental disease affecting children. There is a federal lead paint disclosure act. Often there is a state act that might be more stringent. One such state is Massachusetts – the Childhood Lead Poisoning Prevention Program (CLPPP).

A seller must disclose known instances of lead paint under federal law and some state laws. They must provide copies of lead paint testing results for homes built before 1978. The federal law allows for a ten-day period for a buyer to conduct a lead-paint test at buyer's expense. Ask you agent for a copy of the lead paint disclosure used in your area.

The federal lead paint act is a disclosure only. There is no national rule for a seller to delead a home or make arrangements with a buyer to help in any way. However, as I mentioned, some states such as Massachusetts, have more involved regulations. In Massachusetts, if a child, age six or younger, lives in the home or is going to live in the home, it has to be deleaded. And, it is the buyer who has the responsibility to do the deleading. The seller doesn't have to get involved in it or provide a credit to the buyer.

It is up to the buyer to decide if they want to test for lead paint or not. In a state, such as Massachusetts, you may want to test for lead as it is the buyer's responsibility to deal with the lead in the home if there is a child under age 6.

In general, if the home was built prior to 1978, chances are there is lead paint somewhere in the interior or on the exterior of the home. Buyers often assume that there is lead paint in the house and don't test for it. Usually the layer of paint that has the lead in it has been repainted over several times such that the lead paint is sealed. However, if there is peeling or chipping paint, you need to understand it could contain lead and thus should be repainted. This could be a health hazard in particular if you have children under the age of six who might chew on the chips.

Another caution. If there is peeling or chipping paint, scrapping it or sanding it sends lead particles and dust into the air. That creates a big hazard not only for children but also for pets. The EPA website provides a number of suggestions with regard to remodeling when there is the potential for lead paint.

I knew of a couple with a cat who were living in an older home they were remodeling. They were stripping paint off of doors, doorways, and windowsills. This created a lead-filled dust that the cat was licking and removing from its fur. The cat, unfortunately, died of lead poisoning. Lead paint issues do impact both humans and pets.

- **Mold Testing:** https://www.epa.gov/mold.

From the EPA.gov website:

"Molds are usually not a problem indoors unless mold spores land on a wet or damp spot and begin growing. Molds have the potential to cause health problems. Molds produce allergens (substances that can cause allergic reactions) and irritants. Avoid inhaling or touching mold or mold spores. This may cause allergic reactions in sensitive individuals.

Allergic responses include hay fever-type symptoms. This includes sneezing, runny nose, red eyes, and skin rash. There are potential health effects and symptoms associated with mold exposures. These include allergic reactions, asthma, and other respiratory complaints.

There is no practical way to end all mold and mold spores in the indoor environment. The way to control indoor mold growth is to control moisture. Fix the source of the water problem or leak to prevent mold growth.

Reduce indoor humidity (to from thirty to sixty percent) to decrease mold growth. Some suggestions include venting bathrooms, dryers, and other moisture-generating sources to the outside. Also using air conditioners and de-humidifiers, increasing ventilation. And using exhaust fans whenever cooking, dishwashing, and cleaning."

Mold testing is available for surface testing and air testing. Talk to your agent and home inspector for more information and guidance.

- Chimney Cleaning and Inspection:

From The Chimney Safety Institute of America's website:

"The primary job of a chimney service professional is to aid in the prevention of fires. These include fireplaces, wood stoves, gas, oil and coal heating systems. As well as the chimneys that serve them.

Chimney sweeps install, clean, and maintain systems. They check their performance and prescribe changes to improve their performance. They also educate the consumer about their safe and efficient operation."

More information is available at the CSIA.org website under "Homeowner Resources".

https://www.csia.org/homeowners.html

I'll add some personal observations:

High-efficiency furnaces vent out the sidewall of the basement instead of a chimney. A gas or oil-fired hot water tank sometimes remains vented out the original chimney. Often the hot water tank has difficulty operating in a safe manner. The exhaust enters the basement rather than drafting up the chimney. The hot water tank may need removing from the chimney. They are often replaced with either an electric or high efficiency hot water tank. Or, installing a smaller diameter liner in the chimney can solve the issue.

The crowns of chimneys in older homes often need repointing where gaps are showing. In some cases the entire chimney needs to be rebuilt from the roof up. In some rare circumstances the chimney needs to be rebuilt from the attic floor up. These are very expensive repairs and you should have a good idea of what they cost before buying a home. Or, at least know the cost and negotiate with the seller to help with the repairs.

A client of mine bought a home that needed the chimney rebuilt from the attic floor up through the roof. It was a health and safety issue. We negotiated for the seller to make the repairs at their expense before closing.

- Furnace Cleaning and Inspection:

Heating systems generally come in three different configurations. Electric baseboard or wall heating units. Hot water boiler or steam radiators/baseboard heat. Forced air systems.

Electric baseboard systems tend to be expensive to operate. These are usually tested as part of a general home inspection. They are either controlled by a wall or on-the-unit thermostat. The home inspector turns the thermostat higher and then checks each unit to see if they are working.

Hot water or steam boiler systems are generally oil, gas or propane fired. The combustion area heats up water that either turns to steam or remains as water. Distribution then takes place throughout a home to baseboard or radiator units. In the case of steam radiators, the temperature control is usually on each unit. But, it also includes a thermostat control for the entire system. For hot water systems, a home is often separated into zones, for example by floor. Then separate thermostats control the temperature in each zone.

Both of the above systems provide a "radiant" heat. The forced air heating systems noted below, as their name implies, use a fan to blow air into a room. Many people prefer the radiant heat as air isn't forced into a room. Instead, the heat radiates out of the heating units in the room.

Forced air furnaces circulate air heated in an oil, propane, gas, or wood fired furnace. A "heat exchanger" allows heated air to circulate throughout the home. The exception is an electric based forced air furnace which often uses a heat pump as well to save on energy costs.

Older furnaces had heat exchangers made out of cast iron. These were very thick but not very energy efficient. But they lasted for a long time. Modern forced air furnaces use a thinner, more efficient material. But these heat exchangers sometimes don't hold up. In either case, cracks in the heat exchanger would allow toxic gases to enter your living space. This can produce life-threatening situations. This is different with boiler systems. If these heat exchangers crack the only result would be a puddle on the floor under the boiler. No air is being circulated throughout the home. Instead either hot water or steam is being circulated.

More information can be found here: https://smarterhouse.org/heating-systems/types-heating-systems

- Carbon Monoxide Detectors:

For a home heated by oil, propane, gas or wood, there is a need for carbon monoxide detectors. Place these throughout the living space in the home. These notify occupants if toxic gases are present. Some states, such as Massachusetts, have a smoke and carbon monoxide detector regulation. The local fire department inspects a home for compliance with the regulations. Often, a seller arranges for the inspection and obtains the required compliance certificate. They do this as part of the seller's responsibility before closing.

But, in many states there is no such rule. Fire safety, as well as carbon monoxide poisoning prevention are very important. Give serious consideration to these when you buy a home.

The National Fire Prevention Association's website, https://www.nfpa.org/Public-Education, will provide you with more information.

On fire safety.

"We can all help make the world a safer place by learning more about how and why fires start. We offer countless safety tips on a wide range of timely and important topics. Things you need to know to keep you, your family, and your neighbors safe from fire and related hazards."

The Centers for Disease Control and Prevention, www.cdc.gov, has information about carbon monoxide poisoning.

https://www.cdc.gov/co/default.htm

"Carbon monoxide (CO), is an odorless, colorless gas, which can cause sudden illness and death. It occurs with the burning of a fossil fuel. CDC works with national, state, and local partners to raise awareness about CO. They track, test, and present CO-related illness and death surveillance data in the U.S."

Regardless of the age of the furnace, consider having it cleaned and inspected. This should be part of your inspection contingency.

Hire an unbiased heating contractor to clean and inspect the furnace. This is at the buyer's expense. This is to make sure the furnace operates in an efficient manner. You need to make sure it doesn't have small cracks in the heat exchanger that could lead to major cracks. Major cracks would allow toxic gases to circulate throughout the living space. If there are unsafe cracks, renegotiate your contract. Cracked heat exchangers sometimes are under warranty. Otherwise ask for a credit towards a new furnace. I have seen one-year-old furnaces with cracks developing in the heat exchanger.

- Wood-Damaging Pest (termite) Inspection:

You should have a termite inspection done. This also checks for other wood damaging insects. These include carpenter bees and carpenter ants, as well as powder post beetles.

Usually one will see some evidence of insect pests such as saw dust. You may also see holes in fascia boards where woodpeckers have poked holes in the wood trying to get to ants or bees.

Accurate identification of insect pests is essential to effective control. This is especially critical when wood-damaging insects invade your property. The U.S. Environmental Protection Agency estimates that more than two billion dollars is spent annually on treating wood-damaging pests. While other insects can be nuisances, wood-damaging pests compromise the structural integrity and value of your home. How To Identify And Kill Wood-damaging Pests:

https://www.amdro.com/learn/wood-damaging-pests/identifying-wood-damaging-pests

- Swimming Pool Inspection:

If there is a swimming pool and you intend to use it, have a pool company inspect the pool if it is open and operating. If it isn't open, ask when it was last opened and if closed by a pool company. If it is out of season for pool use, you may have to take the pool as is and hope it works. If a pool specialist closed it the previous season, chances are it will be okay. For more information:

https://www.swimuniversity.com/pool-maintenance/

- Well Testing:

If the property has a well, get the water tested for iron, mineral content, sulfur, and bacteria. You may also want to test it's rate of flow and pressure. Bacteria should be immediately addressed. High iron content can stain plumbing fixtures and clothes. High sulfur content can produce foul-tasting water and foul smells.

Water filtration systems are available to manage such issues, including removal of bacteria. Visit: https://www.culligan.com/blog for more information on water issues and solutions.

- Septic Inspection and Certification:

Some states have stringent requirements with regard to private waste disposal systems. These are also known as a septic system. They may need special inspections and actions. This is to make sure they are in compliance with the local board of health regulations.

If a home has a private septic system, you need to have it inspected. Bringing a septic system up to today's code could cost thousands of dollars.

For information about how a septic tank works check out: https://www.epa.gov/septic.

Make sure also that the system was certified for the number of bedrooms that are actually in the home. If the certification says it is for three bedrooms and there are four bedrooms the system doesn't meet code. You may be paying for a home with four bedrooms that only allows for three-bedroom use.

The usual issues that my clients have found are missing or broken baffles in the tank itself. Or, deteriorated distribution boxes. Renegotiate your contract and have the seller pay for any repairs before closing.

Renegotiate Your Contract if You Find Issues.

An offer contingent upon testing and inspections gives you leverage to re-negotiate.

You should have the option to cancel the contract and receive a refund of your deposit. If the seller does not make a repair or agree to a repair credit you can cancel. You will lose the money spent on the inspections but not your deposit. But, make sure you cancel before the time limit of the inspection contingency.

If your contract gets canceled, it puts pressure on the listing agent. They have to consider problems with the home when attempting to sell it to someone else. Once an agent knows about a problem in the home they must disclose it. Most state laws force an agent and many force a seller, to disclose known issues. They must share known issues with all future prospective buyers. The seller may prefer to work out a deal with you rather than go through the whole process with another buyer.

In a hot market area, expect competing buyers to waive inspection contingencies. Their traditional real estate salesperson pushes for this. They claim their offer will be more attractive by skipping the inspection contingency. You shouldn't take on the risk of unknown problems with the home that you're stuck with after closing. Play it safe. Include the inspection contingency. If the seller accepts another offer, move on to another home. You may have avoided a money pit.

Chapter Eleven
Knowing What Other Contingencies
to Include in Your Offer

Most "fill-in-the-blank" offers to buy real estate are neutral or in favor of the seller.

A buyer needs to write an offer from their perspective. It should have contingencies in it to protect the buyer. Consult with your agent and your attorney to see which contingencies apply to your area.

Eleven important contract contingencies helpful for a buyer:

- Buyer Attorney's Involvement and Review:

Most states restrict a real estate licensee's duties to real estate. They are not allowed to write contracts or make changes to contracts. This restricts them from practicing law. Ask your agent about what involvement an attorney has in your area. Buying a home involves a lot of legal issues. These may need the services of a knowledgeable real estate lawyer. Include a contingency for an attorney's review and approval of the offer if that is applicable in your area.

- Engineer/Property Inspection:

Discussed in chapter ten. It is prudent to have a professional home inspection.

- Other Structural and Mechanical System Inspections:

Also discussed in chapter ten. Professional home inspections are general in nature, and extra testing may be applicable.

- Obtaining Financing and Mortgage Commitment:

You should have gotten a strong bank qualifying letter. Yet, your offer needs to state that it is subject to obtaining financing that is satisfactory to you. What if the interest rate rises so that you no longer qualify? You need a way to get out of the contract if your financing falls through. Make sure there is a mortgage contingency clause so that you get your contract deposit back if you don't qualify.

- Bank Appraisal Equal To or Greater than Sale Price:

In a tight market many homes are selling for asking price or more. It is important that the bank appraisal be equal to or greater than the sale price. A lender bases the mortgage on the lower of the sale price or the appraised value. If the home appraises for less than sale price, you must pay the difference in cash, which you may not have.

By including this contingency, you can renegotiate the price or cancel the transaction. It allows you to get your deposit back if you cancel.

- Receipt and Approval of a Completed Seller's Statement of Property Condition:

This was also discussed in chapter ten. If possible, get the seller to fill one out or work with the disclosure as a negotiation technique.

- Pre-Closing Possession by the Buyer, If Applicable:

Sometimes a buyer's position involves the need to move into the home before closing. What if a buyer has a lease that expires before the closing date on the new home. The buyer doesn't want to move twice. Is the seller's home vacant? You could make arrangements with the seller to move into the home before it closes, and you own it. This would need special provisions in the contract. This may need an attorney's involvement.

- Sale of a Property Owned by the Buyer, if applicable:

Sometimes a buyer has a home to sell so they can buy another home. If they have the cash to buy without selling this isn't a problem. It is an issue if their mortgage needs the sale to qualify. Make the offer subject to the buyer closing the sale on their home before closing on the new home. Sellers would prefer not to sign such an offer but will if the price is right and no competing offers are coming in. But be aware that the seller might want a "bump" provision that would allow them to accept another offer without a home sale contingency.

They would then force you to remove your home sale contingency or loose the deal.

- Subject to Receipt and approval of a Comprehensive Loss Underwriting Exchange (CLUE) Report:

Make your offer subject to the seller obtaining and providing a CLUE report. This is rarely used but if a seller is OK with it, there are advantages to you.

What is CLUE report? CLUE is a claims-information report generated by LexisNexis*(R)*, a consumer-reporting agency. The report usually contains up to seven years of personal-property claims history. Insurance companies report claims which they approve and pay out money, set up a file, or deny a claim.

How do insurance companies use CLUE reports? An insurer may request a CLUE report when you apply for coverage or request a quote. The company reviews your claims history or the history of claims at a specific property. They decide if the company will offer you coverage and at what premium. Studies show a relationship between past claims and claims you report in the future.

A buyer can't get the report for the prospective home and must request that the seller provide it. The Fair Credit Reporting Act entitles an owner to a free annual copy of the CLUE report. More information is available online:

https://www.insurance.wa.gov/clue-comprehensive-loss-underwriting-exchange

You should ask for the report for two reasons. First, you want to see if any past claims will have an impact on your ability to get insurance. Or, on the price you will end up paying. Second, you want to see if there were claims you should review with your home inspector. Then he or she can look at the specific area(s) of the home where damage took place. Such claims could be for fire damage, water damage, wind damage, or other physical matter. These are all things that you should know about.

- Subject to the Signing of a Truth in Lending in Real Estate (TRID) Rider:

A TRID Rider is a TILA-RESPA Integrated Disclosure, now part of any real estate closing. TILA stands for Truth in Lending Act. RESPA stands for Real Estate Settlement Procedures Act.

Delays can occur when the requirements of TRID rules and regulations aren't met on time. The rider provides for extension of time periods to meet TRID requirements. Ask you agent or attorney to provide you with a copy. Here is a further description:

https://kglegal.com/2016/01/know-before-you-owe-trid-rider/

- Closing Cost (Seller Concession) Credits:

Discussed in chapter two. It is important to estimate the amount of cash you need for closing. Then include any request for a seller credit for closing costs in the offer to buy.

Chapter Twelve
Continuing to Check and Follow Up

The closing date indicated in a contract is a target date.

Too many buyers and sellers assume that the closing will take place on the projected date. Very rarely does it happen.

Successful closings need someone who monitors and follows up with the transaction.

Eleven action items that need attention for a successful home closing.

- The appraisal gets done on time.

- The appraised value of the home at least equals the sale price. If not, you and the seller should renegotiate the price down to the appraised amount. If you do not wish to continue, you can cancel the contract.

- The appraiser and lender aren't requiring repairs as part of the mortgage.

- You and the seller agree who will do which repairs, if any.

- Repairs get done and are re-inspected in timely manner.

- A written mortgage commitment gets issued on time.

- No contingencies of the mortgage commitment remain.

- The seller's attorney has located the abstract of title, sent it for re-dating if that applies for your area. Or, ordered the survey, if that applies for your area.

- Your attorney has reviewed title documents and proposed deed and approved of them. Or, has asked the seller's attorney to revise the title document. You want to get unchallengeable ownership of the property.

- A prospective closing time and date that work with your schedule.

- You have an insurance binder. It has a proper mortgagee clause. You've paid one full year's premium and delivered a copy to the closing agent and the lender.

- The closing documents get delivered on time. You get the closing disclosure within three business days before the closing date.

Sound confusing and time consuming?

You bet. And every step needs monitoring to have a closing on or near the anticipated closing date. Lots of disappointments result because no one monitored the process.

Most buyers don't know what transpires in closing on a house. Thus buyers should not be the ones monitoring the process. Of course if no one coordinates the process, the buyer will have to or face not closing on time.

It isn't good enough to contact your attorney or your lender. They may say everything is under control and not to worry. But it may not be. Make sure you have a single professional keeping track of the process.

Your real estate agent should do it. Ask him or her if they will stay on top of things and communicate with you throughout the process.

I see myself as the orchestra conductor. I know everyone's role and when they should perform. I keep the process humming along and under control. Make sure that your agent agrees in advance to watch and track the closing process. Otherwise you may end up disappointed.

Title Insurance:

A quick word about title insurance. A mortgage company will need a lender's title insurance policy covering it as lender. This protects its interest in the event a concern comes up later that clouds title to the property.

Most title matters are resolvable but need an attorney's involvement. The lender's title insurance pays for the attorney and other legal costs to clear the title. What if the issue isn't fixed and the property is unsalable? The title insurance company will then reimburse the bank for the amount of the mortgage. But you will lose any equity you may have in the property.

There is a title policy that protects your equity in the property, an owner's, or fee title insurance policy. It is a one-time fee due at closing. It protects you from undiscovered title defects during your ownership. It also protects you after you sell should a title problem become known after you have sold and moved.

Most attorneys recommend it, and I do, too. Your attorney can explain it in more detail and provide an estimate of the cost. Discuss the pros and cons of title insurance with your attorney before closing.

More information is available at the First American Title website:

https://www.firstam.com/ownership/videos/what-is-title-insurance/

Title Wording:

Another thing to discuss with your attorney before closing is how to take title of the property. This will vary depending on the area in which you are buying. For two or more buyers or a married couple, there may be several available options. Three such options go by the names: tenants in common; joint tenants; tenants by the entirety. Ask your attorney to explain the differences to you and help you decide on your best option. More information is available here:

https://www.investopedia.com/articles/mortgages-real-estate/08/title-ownership-property.asp

Homestead Exemption:

Another thing to ask your agent or attorney about is a homestead exemption. In some states this provides a discount on your real estate taxes. In other states it refers to a method to protect the equity in your home from your creditors. More information is available also at:

https://www.investopedia.com/terms/h/homestead-exemption.asp

Chapter Thirteen
Preparing for and Foreseeing Problems at Closing Time

Are all contingencies in the contract cleared?

Is all paperwork and are title searches completed? You are ready to proceed with a closing where you exchange money for a deed to the home.

There still is much to do once the closing date is set.

- Homeowner's Insurance: You get an insurance binder for your homeowners insurance. You pay a full year's insurance premium in advance and get a receipt for the payment. Then have copies faxed to your attorney. This usually happens before a closing date can be set. The insurance company will need a "mortgagee clause". Look for this information in your mortgage commitment. This is a clause in the insurance that protects and names the lender as an insured in the event of a loss.

Start shopping early for homeowner's insurance. Don't wait until you have a mortgage commitment. Check with the insurance company that insures your car. They may offer a discount for combining your home and auto.

But there is a possibility you will have difficulty obtaining insurance on your new home. This is rare but happens when there were a lot of claims by previous owners. This shows up in the results of a CLUE report, as discussed in chapter eleven. Better to determine if there will be a problem early. Your insurance carrier may pull a CLUE report as part of an application. That gives you time in which to deal with an issue if there is one. Also, your insurance agent may be able to get a CLUE report if the seller isn't willing to provide it to you.

- Utilities: You need to call utility companies, as applicable, to transfer service into your name. These include phone, cable, and internet access. As well as gas, electric, propane, and fuel oil. Also, refuse collection and water. Do this as soon as you know a closing date. You need to take on the financial responsibility for these services as of the closing date. The seller will be cancelling their service. I've had clients inconvenienced for not doing this. They got to their new home and found the utilities turned off. They then experienced a day or two without electric as they waited to have it turned back on.

- Final Inspection: Next comes the final walk-through inspection. This takes place shortly before closing. This is the final opportunity for you to see the home you are buying.

Use the final walk-through inspection to:

- Make sure that the home remained in the condition it was when you entered into the contract to buy it.

- Check for water leaks, damage from movers, yard damage from storms or other events.

- Make sure personal property such as appliances included in the sale are still there.

- Check for instruction booklets for appliances and mechanical systems.

- Make sure remote garage door openers remain.

- Assure that a set of keys will be at closing for you.

- Check utility meter reads. Were they called in? Are utilities in your name? Check the fuel oil tank or propane tank levels. Are these accurate when compared to the reads used to reimburse the seller?

Review of the Closing Disclosure:

Part of the closing process involves a review of a preliminary Closing Disclosure. Compare the Loan Estimate figures with the figures on the Closing Disclosure. We discussed the Loan Estimate in chapter seven. Make sure that items don't appear on the Closing Disclosure that didn't appear on the loan estimate. Review the individual items with your lender in the event there are discrepancies.

There is a Closing Disclosure Explainer online:

http://www.consumerfinance.gov/owning-a-home/closing-disclosure

You should use this to double-check that all the details about your loan are correct.

Lenders must provide your closing disclosure three business days before your scheduled closing. Use the days to resolve problems. If something looks different from what you expected, ask why. Actual costs at closing should be very close to the estimates. Often, differences are accidental. You should have time to get them corrected before closing.

Trying to get a bank to refund money after the fact will be frustrating. You can't get things changed at closing unless they are minor. Making changes on the Closing Disclosure will result in rescheduling the closing. A revised Closing Disclosure means a new three-day period before a rescheduled closing.

Know What Items to Bring to Closing, Including

- A cashier's check payable according to your attorney's instructions. This should include the amount needed to close less your deposit and closing credits.

- Your driver's licenses or other photo identification to verify your identity

- The original insurance binder and paid receipt for reference if needed.

- Your mortgage commitment and lender loan estimate for reference if needed.

- Scam Warning: You may receive an email or letter directing you to send money for the closing to a closing agent. Always question and verify requests for deposits or wiring instructions. Call your agent and/or attorney to make sure that such requests are legitimate.

Chapter Fourteen
Closing and Moving-In

The Actual Closing:

The closing should be a breeze. If someone has monitored the process. If someone has helped you prepare for the closing. If someone has reviewed the closing disclosure with you.

Many times, good preparation isn't done in advance of closing. Some matters often remain to settle at closing. And closings often become battlegrounds. It helps to have a professional, knowledgeable agent working only for you at the closing. They make sure that all goes well. With preparation, the right agent, and right attorney, closings may take less than an hour.

- Real estate closings may take place at the lender's attorney's offices. Or at your attorney's office. Sometimes at the lender's office. Or at the local county clerk's office. And, sometimes at a real estate office. Usually, it takes place wherever it is most convenient for all parties.

- Sellers can sign papers in advance, and some do. Others come to the closing.

- The buyer has to come to a closing to sign the mortgage and other documents. Others there are the buyer's attorney and their agent. Sometimes the seller's attorney and seller's agent are there as well.

- Professional buyer's agents do attend closings. They track the process leading up to the closing. In general they do whatever needs doing to ensure a smooth transaction.

- Make sure you get copies of all signed documents from the closing. This includes temporary payment coupons for your mortgage payment. Your lender may not get your payment coupon book to you on time. You are still required to make payments when due.

- Temporary coupons make it easier for you in the event there is a delay getting the official coupon book to you.

- At closing, you may have the opportunity to sign up for automatic withdrawal of funds to make the payment. It is wise not to sign up at the time of the closing but rather later. You should make several payments to make sure all documentation is accurate. You can sign up for automatic payments at any time, so wait a month or two before you decide to do that.

- Also wait to set up bi-weekly mortgage payments if applicable. Wait a month or two and then contact the lender to make arrangements if you want.

After the Closing:

You can celebrate. You did it. You own your own home. Congratulations. But wait. There are still some things you need to do now that you have closed.

- You should immediately go to your new home to make sure everything is okay. Has anything changed since your walk-through inspection before closing? If anything material has changed, contact your attorney and your agent immediately. Your attorney may be able to put the recording of the deed on hold. That gives time to work things out. Holding up the recording pressures the seller to make things right. If they don't, they risk not receiving the sale proceeds. I've had situations like this happen. A seller came in after our final inspection and took the appliances. I've had neighbors take items they felt were theirs. These situations had happy endings because we were able to put pressure on the seller.

- Make sure you do a change of address with the USPS.

You can make address changes online at the USPS website:

https://moversguide.usps.com/mgo/disclaimer?referral=MG82

It will cost you a dollar charged to a credit card to verify your identity. You can also go to a local postal service office and ask for the USPS moving kit. You need to contact credit card companies and other vendors you do business with. Provide them with your address change.

- You should also as soon as possible re-key all locks in the home. You have no way of knowing who has keys to the property. Until you re-key locks, you are vulnerable to someone using a key to gain unsanctioned access to your home.

- You should also check on the utilities to make sure they are in your name. Make sure you cancel the utilities at your former house.

My sincere wish is that your homebuying adventure is in fact enjoyable.

I hope it is successful and without the drama that sometimes takes place.

And most of all, my goal in writing this book is that you don't get sold a home. I hope you end up buying the right home at the right price and on the right terms.

- Follow your gut.

- Try to keep emotions out of the equation.

- Surround yourself with professionals who care and commit to being true fiduciaries.

Work with an agent who will protect you and look out for your best interest at all times and in every situation. This will guarantee your homebuying adventure will be most enjoyable and successful.

Thank you for reading my book. Please post a review at the retailer where you bought it. Hopefully it will be positive as you found value in reading this book. Email me (tom@tomwemett.com) with any questions or suggestions for future updates to the book.

###

Appendix A
Buying a Home
During a Raging Pandemic
and Economic Crisis

I am writing this book during a health and economic crisis (COVID-19).

I am "sheltering-in-place" at home as many of you are as well at the same time. My real estate business shut down for the time being until it is safe to show homes and attend home inspections.

Chances are the pandemic will still be going on when you are reading this.

Some buyers think that this pandemic is a great time to steal a home. But I don't think that will happen. There was an inventory shortage in most areas when this pandemic began. There is even a greater shortage while we hunker down during this pandemic. Most buyers and sellers are sitting on the sidelines. There still will be an inventory shortage when things get back to normal. That will lead to price stability or increases and not desperate selling.

A National Association of Realtors article came to my attention recently.

It's Title: "Get Ready for a Fast-Evolving Market". It states in part,

"Pent-up housing demand during state shutdowns is about to unleash. There is an easing of many coronavirus-related restrictions to daily life. This is resulting in consumers returning to the real estate market. Home sales are bouncing back from their bottom.

Looking forward, the market is ripe for robust activity. Mortgage applications are defying economists' expectations, rising 54% since April (2020). Mortgage rates for 30-year loans have hit record lows three times in as many months. Borrowing costs favor prospective buyers who are looking to get off the fence and buy. NAR reported a 21.8% drop in pending home sales in April (2020), but says they likely won't go any lower. Meanwhile, home prices continue to rise, even as uncertainty around the pandemic persists."

Throughout most of the country, it is not safe to show a home in-person due to the pandemic.

In some areas it isn't possible and for good reason. I don't know whether I'm infected. My clients don't know if they have the virus or not. We don't know if the seller has the virus. We don't know if the people who viewed the home before us have the virus or were following CDC guidelines. We don't have enough testing. A high percentage of those infected don't have symptoms but yet are able to spread the virus.

And then these remarkable survey statistics.

"Despite the ongoing pandemic risks, 65% of consumers are ready to attend an open house or take a home tour in person."

Also, virtual home sales are increasing. There are people right now during this pandemic buying homes without seeing them. They are relying on online photos and videos. There are real estate sales agents bragging about their virtual sales successes. And this,

"Two of five buyers recently surveyed would buy a home without a visit."

YIKES!

Buying a home without actually seeing it until after you close on it and own it?

Are you kidding? You can't wait twelve to eighteen months to buy a home?

Many sellers "have to" sell their home due to a divorce, a death, or a need to move to another area. That is understandable.

But for buyers, "having to buy" a home is not the same.

- I understand that buyers "want" to buy a home.

- Yes, you want the American Dream of owning your own home.

- Yes, you want to take advantage of the financial and emotional benefits of owning your own home.

- Yes, you want to take advantage of low interest rates.

But, we are in a health and economic crisis none of us has ever experienced.

Stay put!

Need to move...rent for the time being. You will be glad you did.

Relocating? Renting was always my advice to people relocating. Rent and get to know the area. Make sure your new job or adventure works out. Then buy once you are confident about where you want to live.

Home inspections are another issue currently.

The buyer or their agent can't be present in most parts of the country due to the pandemic. Home inspections are being conducted by the inspector alone. No one else may attend. Yes, the inspector takes photos and videos to share with the buyer later.

But these aren't a substitute for the buyer being present at the inspection. My clients find value in the two hours or so they spend face-to-face with the inspector in the home. They feel it is one of the most important aspects of buying a home. Most buyers spend twenty to thirty minutes at most viewing a home before making an offer. So having a two-hour window in which to examine a home in more detail is especially important. Not being able to spend two hours or so face-to-face with a home inspector is a deal breaker for most of my clients.

So here we are.

As I write this book we are in the middle of a pandemic, health crisis that has killed more than 200,000 of us and climbing. Estimates are that the death toll may hit 350,000 or more before this is done. We are in an economic crisis with over 30 million people unemployed. We are also experiencing a social justice crisis. And, in the middle of it all, the traditional real estate industry has their happy faces on. That should give you pause. You may want to reconsider your own personal safety and economic well-being if you are actively out looking to buy a home right now.

Are real estate companies still operating? Of course they are.

Can you view a home in person and stay safe? It depends. Is everyone adhering to strict health crisis guidelines in your area?

Can you buy a home without being present for the home inspection? Yes, although it is a disadvantage for you to do so.

Can you buy a home without seeing it? Yes, virtual sales are booming according to the traditional real estate industry.

But, is there a greater chance of buyer's remorse? Yes!

Is there a greater chance of bidding wars? Yes! And, also a greater chance of loosing money during a real estate bubble. These are well under way in many parts of the country and only made worse due to the pandemic and economic crisis.

Real Estate Companies Seek Indemnification During Bidding Wars:

It recently came to my attention that a large regional real estate association came up with an indemnification form for their members. Its title, "*Potential Adverse Consequence Acknowledgement*". The top of the form has a place for the property address as well as the buyers' names, the buyer agent's name and the buyer agent's broker's name. Then it states,

"We, the undersigned, have decided to submit an offer on the above referenced property. In order to submit a more attractive offer to the seller, certain decisions have been made regarding the terms of our offer as identified by our initials below. We have been advised and fully informed of the

potential adverse consequences that may result from our decisions. The risks of these decisions are understood and we hereby release our Agent, Broker or any agents, subagents or employees of Broker from any liability, loss, damage or adverse consequences that may result from our decisions."

I'll list the specific items below, but understand what is happening here. Several real estate salespeople working with different buyers are advising their buyers to waive all kinds of protective contingencies so that they have a better chance of making a sale and a commission. For sure, it isn't about protecting the buyer. I add contingencies to protect a buyer. I don't push my buyer clients to waive contingencies. Then to add insult to injury, these salespeople ask the buyer to indemnify them from being sued for giving the buyer bad advice. I hope you don't fall for any of these. Wait the market out. The bubble will burst and then you will be able to step in and buy right.

Here are some of the contingencies they advise buyers to waive or approve:

- Offer price higher than the listed price.

- Include price escalation clause in offer.

- Waive financing contingency.

- Waive appraisal contingency.

- Waive home inspection contingency.

- Waive radon test contingency.

- Waive lead-based paint test contingency.

- Waive private well and septic contingency.

- Waive sale/settlement/lease of home contingency.

- Waive termite and wood-destroying insects inspections.

- Accept property subject to additional "AS IS" provisions.

- Buyer has not toured Property in person.

While not all of these are necessary to include in all offers, most are. Waiving these options and then waiving your rights to sue the real estate licensee for bad advice is awful. Please use extreme caution if you are tempted to do any of this.

It is my opinion that you should avoid the hype.

Wait the market out until this pandemic is under control and some normalcy has returned to our lives. It is not worth risking your life to buy a home.

Homes for sale will still be there when the pandemic is finally under control.

Interest rates will remain low to encourage buyers to buy.

The market will have calmed down and stabilized a bit.

Take the time now to:

- Build up your reserves/emergency funds.

- Pay off some of your debt.

- Improve your credit scores.

- Increase your down payment/closing costs fund.

Still want to buy virtually?

If you are still contemplating buying a home virtually, this recent article on Bankrate.com might help. Note that the agent the buyer used was a True Loyal Agent(R), exclusive buyer agent. It you are going to take a chance on buying a home virtually, at least make sure the agent you are using as your buyer agent truly is looking out for your best interest.

https://www.bankrate.com/real-estate/best-practices-for-virtual-homebuying/

Be safe. Stay healthy. Avoid buyer's remorse.

Appendix B
Resources
Link Summary

From the Copyright Page.

- Contact Tom Wemett. 978-248-9898 Email: tom@tomwemett.com

From the Introduction.

- A recent bankrate.com survey of homeowners produced some shocking results.

https://www.bankrate.com/mortgages/homebuyers-survey-february-2019/

- Here is some good advice to start with from Allan Roth, a Financial Planner. It is from an article at aarp.org on August 8, 2016.

https://www.aarp.org/money/investing/info-2016/how-to-make-better-financial-choices-ar.html

From Chapter One - Renting vs. Owning.

- As reported at keepcurrentmatters.com, The Net Worth of a Homeowner is 44x Greater Than A Renter!

https://www.keepingcurrentmatters.com/2018/08/20/the-net-worth-of-a-homeowner-is-44x-greater-than-a-renter/

From Chapter Two - Do You Have Enough Cash for a Down Payment and Closing Costs?

- "Barriers to Accessing Homeownership - Down Payment, Credit, and Affordability – September 2018".

https://www.urban.org/research/publication/barriers-accessing-homeownership-down-payment-credit-and-affordability-2018

(Click on the button to the right to download the 32 page "*pdf*" file.)

- Do you qualify for special down payment or closing cost programs? Check out my link to down payment sources nationally - www.down-payment-finder.com

From Chapter Three - Do You Have Credit Issues or Are Your Credit Scores Too Low?

- "Barriers to Accessing Homeownership - Down Payment, Credit, and Affordability – September 2018"

https://www.urban.org/research/publication/barriers-accessing-homeownership-down-payment-credit-and-affordability-2018

(Click on the button to the right to download the 32 page "*pdf*" file.)

- From the USPIRG, US Public Interest Research Group, "The most valuable thing we have is our good name."

https://uspirg.org/news/usf/new-report-analyzes-complaints-about-credit-bureaus

https://uspirgedfund.org/reports/usf/big-credit-bureaus-big-mistakes

- From a 2012 Federal Trade Commission study mandated by Congress. "One in five consumers has an error in at least one of three major credit reports

https://www.ftc.gov/news-events/press-releases/2015/01/ftc-issues-follow-study-credit-report-accuracy

- For more information about credit reporting and credit scores go to the MyFico.com website.

https://www.myfico.com/credit-education

- The three major credit bureaus and their contact information are:

EQUIFAX - https://www.equifax.com/personal/

EXPERIAN - https://www.experian.com/

TRANSUNION - https://www.transunion.com/

- The Fair and Accurate Credit Transactions Act of 2003—the FACT Act. This requires credit bureaus to provide one free credit report every twelve months. The official web site is: www.annualcreditreport.com.

https://www.annualcreditreport.com/index.action

- More information is available on the Federal Trade Commission's web site.

https://www.ftc.gov/. Click on the Get Your Free Credit Report button on the right side

- The CFPB is an excellent source of information about credit and homebuying. Navigate to the CFPB consumer website.

https://www.consumerfinance.gov/. Then check under Consumer Tools (Located in the top menu on the far left) for more information about financial related subjects.

- You can buy all three credit reports and FICO scores at www.myfico.com/

https://www.myfico.com/.

- The Consumer Financial Protection Bureau issued a warning. "How to tell a reputable credit counselor from a bogus credit repair company."

https://www.consumerfinance.gov/ask-cfpb/how-can-i-tell-a-credit-repair-scam-from-a-reputable-credit-counselor-en-1343/

From Chapter Four - Will You be Able to Find a Home You Like Within Your Budget?

- "Barriers to Accessing Homeownership - Down Payment, Credit, and Affordability – September 2018"

https://www.urban.org/research/publication/barriers-accessing-homeownership-down-payment-credit-and-affordability-2018

(Click on the button to the right to download the 32 page "*pdf*" file.)

- Use one of the online rent-vs-buy calculators. I like the one available from NerdWallet.com. https://www.nerdwallet.com/mortgages/rent-vs-buy-calculator.

- Your Home Vision Checklist. I have made this available on my website to help with the step of determining your home vision. This file is from my own secure and trusted website. https://make-better-homebuying-decisions.com/wp-content/uploads/2020/07/Your-Home-Vision-Checklist.pdf

- What school district? Check out: https://www.greatschools.org/ for information about schools in the area in which you want to live.

- There are many mortgage calculators online today. One such calculator I recommend is from NerdWallet: https://www.nerdwallet.com/mortgages/mortgage-calculator/calculate-mortgage-payment?trk=nw_gn1_4.0

- This website will give you the best up-to-date database of listed property anywhere in the country. https://www.realtor.com/.

From Chapter Five - Should You Wait to be in a Better Buying Position?

- **Rent to Own** - People often rent-to-own a TV, a computer or other household goods. It can work also for buying a home. A rent-to-own, also known as a lease/option, agreement allows you to lease a home that you have the "option" to purchase later when you are able.

https://rent-to-own-your-own-home.com/

From Chapter Six - Do You Know Who to Trust and Work With?

- I have an arrangement with a national buyer agent referral service organization. They help buyers find the best buyer agent to use in their area to help them buy their home. Find your best buyer agent at:

https://best-buyer-agent-search.com/

- The Association of Real Estate License Law Officials, ARELLO, lists the real estate commissions by state on their website.

https://www.arello.org/resources/regulatory-agencies/#region1
Locate the state you are buying a home in. Click on the state's website for more information specific to your state.

- There is an excellent article about disclosures by the Consumer Federation of America.

https://consumerfed.org/press_release/new-report-real-estate-disclosures-about-agent-representation-often-lack-key-information-are-too-complex-and-are-not-timely/

"New Report: Real Estate Disclosures about Agent Representation Often Lack Key Information, Are Too Complex, and Are Not Timely".

- Avoid Loan Fraud. Many buyer agents have begun to offer to credit a portion of the real estate commission to their clients. It is not illegal in most states for an agent to offer to pay money to a purchaser as an inducement to have them sign an exclusive agency agreement. However, this practice can lead to other problems for both purchasers and their agents further down the road, particularly at settlement.

https://www.nvar.com/realtors/laws-ethics/legal-blog/debunking-legal-myths-kickback-vs.-rebate

From Chapter Seven - Understanding Mortgage Options and Obtaining a True Mortgage Pre-approval.

- Government-backed programs include those sponsored by the US government. Federal Housing Administration (FHA). Veterans Administration (VA). US Department of Agriculture (USDA) rural area loans.

FHA: https://www.hud.gov/buying/loans

VA: https://www.benefits.va.gov/homeloans/

USDA: https://www.rd.usda.gov/programs-services/single-family-housing-guaranteed-loan-program

- A rule went into effect on October 3, 2015 that requires borrowers must receive a loan estimate. This is part of regulations overseen by the Consumer Financial Protection Bureau-www.cfpb.gov

https://www.consumerfinance.gov/owning-a-home/loan-estimate/

- The APR computation is especially useful for two loans showing different interest rates. The APR computation isn't perfect, but it does give you a basis for comparing loans.

https://www.bankrate.com/glossary/a/apr/

 - APR Calculator - When applying for loans, aside from interest, it is not uncommon for lenders to charge additional fees or points. The real APR, or annual percentage rate, considers these costs as well as the interest rate of a loan. The following two calculators help reveal the true costs of loans through real APR.

https://www.calculator.net/apr-calculator.html

From Chapter Eight - Looking at All Available Homes.

- Special loan programs allow borrowing money to buy the home as well as an amount to fix it up. FHA 203K is one such mortgage program.

https://www.hud.gov/program_offices/housing/sfh/203k/203k--df

   Another such program that allows borrownig money to buy a home as well as an amount to fix it up is the Fannie Mae Homestyle Loan.

Fannie Mae Homestyle Loan:

https://www.lendingtree.com/home/mortgage/complete-guide-to-homestyle-renovation-mortgage/

Compare the two:

https://www.nerdwallet.com/article/mortgages/203k-and-homestyle-mortgage-loans-for-home-renovation

- Property Tax Exemptions: Do You Qualify? You may qualify for a money-saving property tax exemption. Learn about five types of tax relief.

https://www.houselogic.com/finances-taxes/taxes/property-tax-exemptions/

- Challenging Property Taxes. From Forbes, Millions of homeowners have no idea they can actually lower their property taxes. They casually glance -- or grimace -- at their mortgage escrow notice every year and pony up without doing a thing. Despite possible savings of thousands of dollars, only 2% of homeowners appeal their assessments, which is the first step in lowering taxes.

https://www.forbes.com/sites/johnwasik/2018/07/13/how-you-can-save-money-by-appealing-your-property-tax-assessment/#11d80d6075fc

From Chapter Ten - Including Contingencies for Property Inspections.

- There are two national home inspector associations. The American Society of Home Inspectors, ASHI and the National Association of Certified Home Inspectors, NACHI.

You can find report samples and information here.

ASHI: https://www.homeinspector.org

NACHI: https://www.nachi.org/blind.htm

- Consider other inspections and tests that may be applicable to the home you want to buy. These aren't included in most general inspections.

Radon Testing: https://www.epa.gov/radon

Lead Paint Testing: https://www.epa.gov/lead

https://www.epa.gov/lead/protect-your-family-lead-your-home-real-estate-disclosure

Mold Testing: https://www.epa.gov/mold

Chimney Cleaning and Inspection: https://www.csia.org/homeowners.html

Carbon Monoxide Poisoning: The Centers for Disease Control and Prevention has information about carbon monoxide poisoning. https://www.cdc.gov/co/default.htm

Fire Prevention: The National Fire Prevention Association's website will provide you with more information.
https://www.nfpa.org/Public-Education

Wood-Damaging Pest (termite) Inspection: Accurate identification of insect pests is essential to effective control. This is especially critical when wood-damaging insects invade your property. The U.S. Environmental Protection Agency estimates that more than two billion dollars is spent annually on treating wood-damaging pests. While other insects can be nuisances, wood-damaging pests compromise the structural integrity and value of your home.

Three primary pests are behind most insect-related structural damage in the United States are Carpenter Bees; Carpenter Ants; and Termites

Identifying-and-Controlling-Wood-Destroying-Insects:

https://www.amdro.com/learn/wood-damaging-pests/identifying-wood-damaging-pests

Swimming Pool Inspection:

For more information: https://www.swimuniversity.com/pool-maintenance/

Well Testing:

Water filtration systems are available to manage such issues, including removal of bacteria. Visit: https://www.culligan.com/blog for more information on water issues and solutions.

Septic Inspection and Certification:

If a home has a private septic system, you need to have it inspected. Bringing a septic system up to today's code could cost thousands of dollars. For information about how a septic tank works check out:
https://www.epa.gov/septic

From Chapter Eleven - Knowing What Other Contingencies to Include in Your Offer.

- Make your offer subject to the seller obtaining and providing a CLUE report. CLUE is a claims-information report generated by LexisNexis*(R)*, a consumer-reporting agency.

More information is available at:
https://www.insurance.wa.gov/clue-comprehensive-loss-underwriting-exchange

From Chapter Twelve - Continuing to Check and Follow Up.

- Title Insurance: https://www.firstam.com/ownership/videos/what-is-title-insurance/

- How to hold title: https://www.investopedia.com/articles/mortgages-real-estate/08/title-ownership-property.asp

- Homestead Exemption: https://www.investopedia.com/terms/h/homestead-exemption.asp

From Chapter Thirteen - Preparing for and Foreseeing Problems at Closing Time.

- Review of the Closing Disclosure: Part of the closing process involves a review of a preliminary Closing Disclosure. Compare the Loan Estimate figures with the figures on the Closing Disclosure. There is a Closing Disclosure Explainer online.

www.consumerfinance.gov/owning-a-home/closing-disclosure

From Chapter Fourteen - Closing and Moving-in.

- Changing Your Address: https://www.usps.com/ Click on "Quick Tools" and then on "Change My Address".

About the Author

Tom Wemett

Tom Wemett is a nationally known author, instructor, homebuyer representation specialist and real estate investor.

He got his entrepreneurial start as the Secretary/Treasurer for the Wemett Corporation. This was a gas and fuel oil distributorship started by his grandfather, Clarence, in 1906. Located in Hemlock, south of Rochester, NY, it had 4500 fuel oil accounts and 35 gas stations.

The family business sold in 1971 and Tom spent the next two years working for a local investor. He helped the investor buy over $22 million worth of income property in 15 states over 2 1/2 years. He then started his own real estate brokerage and property management firm in 1973. He operated from 1973 to 2004 in the greater Rochester, New York, area.

In the late 1980's, Tom purchased a Help-U-Sell franchise. This business provided special marketing and sales programs for sellers. However, the marketing drew in lots of buyers. Tom and his agents ended up spending more time helping buyers than helping sellers.

It was customary at the time for all real estate licensees to represent sellers but not buyers. Real estate licensees treated buyers as customers. But the real estate company treated sellers as clients. Buyers had no representation. But, sellers did. The phenomenon started to change in the late 1980's. Buyer representation became acceptable and desired by homebuyers.

Tom saw a conflict. He had listings and was looking out for the best interest of these sellers. He realized it would be impossible to look out for the best interest of a buyer of the same property.

For Tom the decision was clear and simple. Represent one side only and end the conflict of interest. He stopped attempting to represent both a seller and a buyer on the same property in the same company. In 1992, Tom became and continues today as an exclusive buyer's agent. He represents homebuyers only and never represents homesellers or takes listings.

Homebuyers want to buy the right home at the right price. Tom's focus is to make sure that happens and has dedicated his real estate career to that goal.

Tom is the founder-broker-manager of Homebuyer Advisers LLC. Tom is a licensed real estate broker in Florida, Massachusetts and New York State.

Tom is the founder-manager of Neighborhood Property Partners LLC. Neighborhood Property Partners LLC is a company that purchases, rehabs, and sells houses. NPP works with motivated sellers who need cash offers as well as investor/partners looking to fix and flip or buy and hold quality homes. More information is available here: https://www.facebook.com/BuySellRentRE/

Tom also helps people buy homes using "Rent-To-Own" programs. You can find out more about renting to own a home at https://rent-to-own-your-own-home.com/

Tom has a BS BA business degree from RIT, the Rochester Institution of Technology. He also has taken the following training and has earned the following certifications.

- Accredited Buyer Representative, ABR

- Accredited Buyer Representative Manager, ABRM

- Certified Exclusive Buyer Agent Master, CEBA-M

- Certified Buyer Representative, CBR

- Certified Buyer Agent, CBA

- Certified Residential Specialist, CRS

- Graduate REALTOR(R) Institute, GRI

- Certified Negotiation Expert, CNE

- Senior Real Estate Specialist, SRES

- Certified New Home Sales Professional, CSP

- Certified Homeowner Educator and Counselor, CHEC.

Tom is available for consultations about real estate homebuying or investing. He can be reached at 978-248-9898 or by email: tom@tomwemett.com

Other Books by Tom Wemett

(Available on Amazon.com)

Massachusetts Homebuyers Beware! The Cards are Stacked Against You.

A thorough guide to prospective homebuyers in Massachusetts with special emphasis on the True Loyal Agent(R) exclusively representing a buyer. The author helps flip the odds in favor of the homebuyer, provides information that will help the homebuyer buy the right home at the right price, and provides the homebuyer with knowledge to enable finding the right agent.

Praise: 5.0 out of 5 stars. **This book is an excellent first step in a complicated process.**

Reviewed in the United States on March 27, 2018: *Buying a home is like buying a car, on steroids. It's the biggest investment you are likely to make so the stakes are incredibly high. I knew that having an agent represent me was a good idea. What I hadn't grasped was how important it is to find one who is not connected with the selling side in any way—through an agency that also represents sellers, as most do, at least in Mass. In researching buyer agents, I found Tom through the Mass. Assoc. of Buyer Agents (MABA). He sent a complimentary copy of his book. We ended up hiring him and he did a great job for us—so we saw his printed words turned to action. I'm a true believer that having someone represent you who has no conflict with the selling side is an absolute must.*

Collaborating Author with Joseph Éamon Cummins.

Not One Dollar More! How to Save $3000 to $30000 Buying Your Next Home

WHY YOU NEED TO READ THIS BOOK: Almost all homebuyers pay too much for their homes - and never discover their misfortune! After all, who's going to tell you? Think about it. Since 1995 this book has helped over 100,000 homebuyers to save money, avoid tricks and traps, buy safely the RIGHT home and get true peace of mind.

UNQUESTIONABLE HONESTY: This book is trusted - because it's honest. The author, a nationally recognized consumer advocate, has NO ties to any realty company or bank. You get NO sales pitch, NO up-sells, NO add-ons, NO guru seminars, NO 'free gifts' that nab your email address. Just priceless advice.

This third edition has new chapters on topics that confuse most homebuyers:

How to: Negotiate persuasively but quietly; Be certain you get the best mortgage; Save thousands in how you repay your home loan; Engage a true agent to guide you through the entire buying process.

Praise: *American Homeowners Foundation (represents America's 70m homeowners) said of the first edition: 'Few book writers can put money into your pocket, here's one who can!'. Tony Robbins said: 'This book is extraordinary!'.*

www.ingramcontent.com/pod-product-compliance
Lightning Source LLC
Chambersburg PA
CBHW060452280326
41933CB00014B/2738